AROUND THE WORLD UNDER 30

A SECRET TO TRAVEL THE WORLD BEFORE YOU TURN 30

DEVESH GOLANI

Contents

Preface

This book is a result of my core philosophies combined with the freedom I had to explore the world at a young age. I am a traveller and not a writer, so this might not be the perfect Preface as per standards but rest assured, my enthusiasm to share my knowledge and inspire young people to travel fearlessly remains the same.

Around the world, travelling young is considered a luxury that only a few people can afford, but with the help of this book, I want to try to break that stereotype and shape the reader's mindset to believe otherwise. I want you to understand the mindset behind travelling young and all the benefits it brings. I want to implore how important or essential it is to travel when we are young and how it shapes our entire life and mindset forever.

Fortunately, I had the early travel opportunity to Australia at the age of 16 for a month-long stay which made me even crazier to travel the world for the rest of my life. With that energy and all the research techniques I learned over time, I was able to travel around 40 countries under the age of 30 without leaving my career or giving up on my family. This book is something very close to me as I have poured my heart out with everything I know.

I hope this book inspires you to explore this beautiful world and everything it has to offer, especially in your prime years when you have greater capabilities and a strong mind.

CHAPTER ONE

There Is No Tomorrow

"Travel like there's no tomorrow, and if tomorrow comes, travel again."

There is no tomorrow. It's easy to go through life, thinking that all of your dreams will come true. That you're going to do that thing that you've wanted to do for years, that you're going to get that job, that you will see that place, that you will travel the world once you have enough money. Whatever that dream is that you're holding in your mind, it's easy to think that you're going to get there just by waiting.

It's easy to put off the actions that will get you to where you want to be and say that you're going to do them tomorrow. "Tomorrow I'll make that call," "Tomorrow I will plan that Europe Trip," "Tomorrow I'll decide if the vacation will be worth it," "Tomorrow is going to be better if I save enough money right now."

Procrastination is a terminal disease. You don't feel it. You can't see it, and no surgery can remove it. But if you let it, it will kill your dreams. Because let me tell you this, you will not be here forever. You're going to Die.

And if you ain't careful, you're going to get to the end of your life and still be saying that you're going to do it tomorrow. THERE IS NO TOMORROW.

From this moment forward, I want you to start living your life as if tomorrow wasn't going to come and that right now, right here, is the only time you can act. Not tomorrow, not next week but right here, right now.

Action. Action is the only cure for procrastination. Do you want to tell that person you love them? Do it Now! Do you want to say sorry? Do it Now! Don't wait. Don't make excuses.

Don't come up with reasons why you can't, and focus on all the shit that might happen if things go wrong. Just get up, get out and get things done! Because one of these days will be your last.

Make sure you did everything you wanted to do, everything you wanted to do in this life. You get one shot. One. Do it. Do it Now!

Every time you find yourself putting things off and procrastinating, I want you to remind yourself that there is no tomorrow. There is only Today for you to act!

Travelling is something that most of us think we can do tomorrow or do once we have enough money, enough time, or maybe enough circumstances to support the crazy passion. But I want to tell you that travelling is not something which needs to be perfect and done with vast money or it's not a luxury as we might prefer to think. I witness too many people making plans for the future to have those plans derailed by unexpected illness and death or viruses.

Unfortunately, I know some people who worked more than 50 hours a week and always thought that there was a better and greater tomorrow when they could do everything they dreamed of, and suddenly Covid-19 took their life at an early age. This is unfair and sad to everyone who thought they were doing the right thing because we never really feel the future is uncertain or unknown to humankind.

My aim here is not to scare you or leave a negative footprint that life is too short. We should take risks to do whatever we think is correct, but instead, my idea is to convince you that living in the moment is very important. This simple change in perspective can lead you to take actions that satisfy you in your current life instead of just hoping for the future without enjoying Today.

Many people accept life without pushing back, without taking the initiative to make their ideal life a reality. Despite popular belief, you do not have to wait years before doing what you want to do.

Delayed gratification is a Myth

In the 1960s, a Stanford professor named Walter Mischel began conducting a series of important psychological studies. During his experiments, Mischel and his team tested hundreds of children — most of them around the ages of 4 and 5 years old.

The experiment began by bringing each child into a private room, sitting them down in a chair, and placing a marshmallow on the table in front of them.

At this point, the researcher offered a deal to the child.

The researcher told the children that he would leave the room and that if the child did not eat the marshmallow while he was away, they would be rewarded with a second marshmallow. However, if the child decided to eat the first one before the researcher returned, they would not get a second marshmallow.

So the choice was simple: one treat right now or two treats later.

The researcher left the room for 15 minutes.

As you can imagine, the footage of the children waiting alone in the room was rather entertaining. Some kids jumped up and ate the first marshmallow as soon as the researcher closed the door. Others wiggled and bounced and scooted in their chairs as they tried to restrain themselves but eventually gave in to temptation a few minutes later. And finally, a few of the children did manage to wait the entire time.

The children who were willing to delay gratification and waited to receive the second marshmallow ended up having higher SAT scores, lower levels of substance abuse, lower likelihood of obesity, better responses to stress, better social skills as reported by their parents, and generally better scores in a range of other life measures.

But how did the children distract themselves? They sang a song or played a game inside their heads. What they did not do was sit there and stare at the marshmallow, vainly attempting to tap into deep reservoirs of self-control or personal discipline.

So we have to ask ourselves: Is "delaying gratification" what the successful kids did? Or did they merely substitute the source of their gratification—switching their focus from something possibly gratifying in the future (more marshmallows) to something immediately satisfying in the present (singing and playing)?

To say that successful kids and adults "delay gratification" misses the point.

When we focus on "not eating the marshmallow," we imply that successful people are those who are better at sucking it up and enduring the pain and struggle necessary to pursue an expected gain some day, week, or a year down the road. Meanwhile, they let all the pleasures of life pass them by.

When we set up the situation this way for our kids, our employees, or ourselves, we present life as a choice between either a) succeed later but be miserable now, or b) enjoy today even though it means sacrificing your future.

Could this be why so many of us toggle back and forth between feeling guilty one minute about our inability to stick with our goals and then the very next minute feeling just as guilty about our inability to "be present" and to "live in the now"? No matter which choice you make, you lose.

The secret to success in the marshmallow test of life and work is not about delaying gratification. It is about discovering gratification in every situation. It's about leveraging the human mind's unparalleled ability to find—and focus on—small sources of gratification in any set of circumstances.

Similarly, many people in life approach Delayed gratification when it comes to enjoying the pleasure of travelling because somewhere, we have been taught that pain and suffering at a young age is the only right thing if we have to enjoy the future.

But unfortunately, Travel is an experience which changes with age. If you are in your early 20s, you can digest any local food globally, but if you are in your 50s, you would be scared to try even the same things in a different country because you never know how your body would react.

People who Live in the Present are Happier

It's a cliche to say that living in the present moment is the key to happiness. But like a lot of cliches, it might contain a kernel of scientific truth.

Psychologists call how you relate to the past, present, and future your time perspective. And according to a recent study, people's time perspectives correlate with life satisfaction, anxiety, and depression.

In the study, researchers from Greece asked 413 participants to complete several surveys looking at the participants' time perspectives and overall wellbeing.

When they looked at the data, it turned out that people who were more satisfied with their lives tended to have a more indulgent attitude toward the present – that is, they were more focused on experiencing pleasure in the present moment.

According to the authors, this finding suggests that "the tendency to take risks and to fulfil one's desires may lead to experiencing pleasure in a 'seize the day' approach to life." You thought carpe diem was just a catchy phrase, but if this research holds up, it might turn out to be a scientific prescription for happiness!

If people who live in the present are more satisfied with life on average, the opposite seems to be true for those who dwell in the past.

That said, it's worth keeping in mind that the researchers weren't looking at which way the causation goes. It could be that living for the present moment makes people happier, or it could just be that being happy makes people more prone to live in the present. Or, quite possibly, some mixture of the two is at play.

Still, it probably can't hurt to look for the little (or big) things we can do to make the present more enjoyable. Seizing the day has rarely made people less satisfied with their lives!

This book will provide insight into ways to think differently about life, focusing on travel, work, health, and finance. The goal is to encourage you to live your life with intent, making the most of every day. I hope you will join along on the journey! Also, at the end of some chapters, I will ask you to complete a few fun exercises which will help you understand yourself better.

Let's Focus Travelling

Travelling means pushing boundaries, exploring, experiencing that extraordinary feeling of freedom—the places you choose where to tell about you, your tastes, characteristics, and aspirations. The love of exploration is also what has led many of us expats to live abroad.

How come we travel?

According to an Australian psychologist, humans are nomads by nature from a primitive point of view. Even though we have evolved, the innate desire to wander is still deeply ingrained in our psyche. Human beings are also naturally curious, and travel allows you to explore and learn about new realities.

There are many psychological concepts concerning travel, and today, I want to deepen some of them here:

The peak experience: You can experience the peak experience when you travel. It can be described as a wave of vitality and euphoria, in which all the senses are more sensitive. The person feels themselves fully and gratified. The peak experience is a sort of internal spark that brings a great sense of awe and wonder and during which the person feels in touch with their life.

The search for sensations: One of man's basic needs is the need to be stimulated: to touch, see, feel, hear, taste. Therefore, the drive to travel is also explained as searching for the satisfaction of this "hunger for stimuli" and sensation seeking. Each person is different and needs a specific amount of stimulation, hence how many activities they decide to undertake and how much they travel.

A place can mean taking a break from what weighs us and focusing on ourselves and what pleases us. In this sense, the desired trip serves to decompress and reduce cortisol, the stress hormone.

When we travel, we are involved in a motion dictated by physical movements and directed by the soul's continuous stresses. This 360-degree participation of our being is at the origin of a series of beneficial changes for our personality.

One of the most frequent reasons why travel is used is to dampen the tension accumulated in our daily lives of commitments, rhythms, and problems of various kinds.

A trip has a therapeutic value in the treatment of stress, as it allows you to escape from that routine which, in the long run, generates in you a solid psychological discomfort, depriving you of the energy necessary to carry on your life. At the end of each trip, you can feel the sensation of having found serenity and reacquired the forces that allow you to return to your habits with a proactive spirit.

Travel is a panacea for body and mind: the relaxing effect that the change of air and environment produces has highly positive repercussions on your body, making the mind more active and brilliant, helping the body regain vigour and beauty, rejuvenating you.

Taking a trip is like leafing through the pages of many books: it deepens our knowledge, broadens our views, makes us more tolerant and sensitive people, and continually stimulates curiosity for the new.

"You were not made to live like brutes, but to follow virtue and knowledge," read Dante's Ulysses, a symbol of man's unstoppable impulse to move, discover, increase his knowledge. Discovering cultures other than ours is the best way to deal with otherness, obtaining an inestimable wealth to be preserved for years to come. We can benefit from everything new when travelling: food, language, religious traditions, typical customs.

Travelling together generates indelible memories, strengthening bonds of friendship, love & affection.

And if it is nice to travel around the world in the company, so is travelling alone: it is an excellent test of courage and strength, thanks to which you learn to get by yourself, to make decisions quickly, to acquire pragmatism, and autonomy. At the end of his adventure, the solitary traveller will be a more mature and responsible person. He will have had the opportunity to converse several times with himself, knowing himself and enjoying solitude as a precious gift.

If you are still sceptical about all the benefits of travelling young, the hope is that this book will convince you to plan a trip as soon as possible, filling your backpack or suitcase and leaving your heart free to store wellbeing, beauty & happiness.

The study led by the university professor of psychology, Thomas Gilovich, wanted to title this experiment "A wonderful life: experiential consumption and the pursuit of happiness" or instead tends to emphasise the importance of spending one's money on a life experience to be able to find happiness, rather than paying one's money on an object. This is because a trip would significantly increase the sense of joy.

Action Items you should complete before moving to the Next Chapter:

● Make a dream travel list that might sound very silly or stupid at the moment, but do it anyway. You never know what power resides in powerful and thoughtful writing.

● If there are no restrictions/visa problems/finance problems, where would You travel in the world right now and why? Note down the answer and think about it.

CHAPTER TWO

Why You Should Travel Young?

So, you must be wondering why I emphasize that travelling younger is much better and more impactful than travelling older. Well, I think travelling at any age is terrific and a learning experience, it's just that we don't know for a fact that we even have tomorrow to live.

When writing this page, the world is in so much pain due to COVID-19, and there are so many deaths everywhere. Deaths of people who were on the verge of retirement, deaths of people who just finished college, deaths from every age, and every caste/religion/ nationality.

The point is that no one in the world knows how much time they are left with, not you, not me, not any astrologer, no one!

What does that leave us with? Just present time and a big fat expectation of the future. We always have been promised a better tomorrow, but for a fact, we have this time, this moment of surety which is now. Thus, instead of making plans for tomorrow, we should concentrate & enjoy the present! One such splendid way is to travel. But you'd ask why travel when there are tons of other ways to enjoy? That's because travelling broadens one's perspective, helps mentally rejuvenate oneself & gains invaluable experiences.

Travelling young is one of the best things you can do because you are not sure of tomorrow, you are not sure that your plan of working hard in your young age and living in old age will even take off for sure. You also grasp and understand hell a lot more at your young age than later.

I think travelling young is one of the best early education you can get, which no school in the world can give you. Sure, you still might need school to know other essential things, but only travelling exposes you to different cultures, different philosophies.

Think of it in just simple terms. Your body and mind are super flexible at an early age to adapt to any challenge thrown at you. You also have way more risk-taking capacity because you don't have much to lose. But if you try to do similar things when you are old, you have to be extra careful, and when you be extra cautious, sometimes it's not enjoyed as much as it could be.

Sure, we can travel anytime but doing it young has the energy to grasp more, enliven it more & enjoy it much. Here's a list of "Why":

To Not Regret

During this pandemic, we've got time to reflect on ourselves. Many of us have realized our actual inner desires, which were otherwise not possible in our 9 to 5 routines or the mundane lives we've lived. This pause was somewhere necessary to understand we don't live to earn &

eat, but earn & eat to live.

On pondering over my job & life, I realized: Indeed, I love my job. I have an incredible job working with individuals I genuinely appreciate, regard, and respect. I like the test of the work and the feeling of achievement it can give. Yet, I don't work since I like it. I work to accommodate my family. I work so we can do things all together that we appreciate.

When travelling for business reasons, you don't always have the opportunity to enjoy the experience fully. But when we leave because we decide and choose the destination, the benefits we can draw are many: from personal growth to psychophysical well-being, from discovering new emotions to new places and people. Thanks to a trip, we can see much more than a city, and the best time to do so is undoubtedly the youth.

Energy & Physical endurance

One of the reasons it's best to travel young is that we would have peak energy levels, be it experiencing scuba diving, paragliding, rafting & all such sporty activities requiring physical strength & ability to handle thrill are only possible when young. You never know if some mismanaged bone movement would stop you from doing all this in the future as you age.

From the science of physiological wellness perspective: At different life stages, our body radiates/reverberates different amounts of energy. That energy exuded is directly proportional to the impact that experience will have on us. Simply put, the same incident happening can have a different response in cases of different time zone, people & the circumstances they are dealing with at that present time. When young we are more energetic & thus the experiences, we would have would be more impactful shaping our overall personality.

If you wait past your 20s to go abroad, it will be more challenging to make that leap. Your twenties are a bolder, gutsier time when you're willing to push your limits to grow. Take advantage of that youthful attitude and go abroad while you have the chance.

Less Responsibilities, More Fun

We all experience the loading of more & more responsibilities & things we need to take care of with burgeoning in life but trust me; you would rarely get that "living care-free" phase besides being under the shelter of parents at a tender age.

As young people, most of us have a pretty established comfort zone. At home with mom and dad, in a community that has known you for probably a good part of your life. You have your established friends, activities, hangouts, and possibly jobs. We become comfortable in these daily roles, and the idea of breaking out can be scary and uncomfortable.

The problem is, you learn the most in uncomfortable, unfamiliar situations. We know how to act and respond to people and our surroundings in our daily routines. Being in a new place, with different people who hold different values and go about life differently (or not so different, you may find) strips all that familiarity away.

It can be scary, but once you figure out that you can connect with people despite differences and navigate foreign environments, you become a more innovative, more competent individual. Going on a trip with someone strengthens the bond: whether friendship or love, the emotions, and memories help enhance the relationship between two people. So, asking someone we care about to take the trip together is a good idea.

By travelling, we can revitalize youth which is often suffocated by daily stress: it has been found that visiting new places can slow down the perception of time by making time seem to pass more slowly. This relaxes us by lowering our stress levels and being much calmer upon our return!

Only with Open, Worry Less minds we can have the best fun. Be it having a yacht party with friends or clubbing or exploratory travel discovering the beauty of historical & wondrous places, Go for them today! (Never cancel Goa Plans with friends, because if not now, could you imagine being there with your friends at 60-70?)

You have all the time in the world

This applies to the most privileged ones: In the early phases of life, we aren't accountable to indulge in formalities, care about our education & enjoy & learn through life. So, sparing us much time daily requires a few time management tricks, but it will indeed be worthy of experiencing new things & exploring different places & people.

A quote from John Steinbeck says: "People don't take trips; it's trips that people take." This phrase is part of one of the reasons why we should travel as young people. When we are at home, we often do not feel free to be ourselves: school, university, work. We feel closed in a particular role, and we cannot reveal what we want to become. A journey takes us away from this reality and forms our identity through a reflective path.

Ask yourself, with a gift as unpredictable and fragile as life, do you have the time for making plans but not go anywhere?

To gain practical knowledge

By travelling, we can learn about the diversity in the world, about different cultures, different people & moreover being comfortable with uncomfortable, going out of our loving home & learning about real life, external world.

Travelling means increasing one's cultural baggage every day, but travelling does not mean having to deprive oneself of conventional studies. Today, thanks to technology, we can study remotely and obtain an online master's degree, for example, without having to give up on discovering the world. Plus, scientists say travelling makes us smarter!

Sometimes it's only far from home that you realize you've got skills you've never used. It's travel that brings them to the surface and makes you smile, satisfied to have reached the mountain top, or crossed a gorge or helped a villager clean up after a storm, or even to have successfully ordered a meal at a rural Chinese restaurant.

The journey opens the mind, allows you to look at the world from another angle, and allows you to face life and problems from another perspective. It is much easier to resolve a situation when we look at it from the outside rather than fully living it. Youth is characterized by uncertainty, fear, plans, and ambitions, and a journey helps to have a clearer vision of one's future. This is an excellent reason for travelling as a young person: choosing the path to take in life is not always easy, and a vacation allows you to look inside yourself and understand more clearly what is best to do.

Making this world look like a small place

Travelling teaches you a lot about the world and yourself. After taking an extended time to travel, you'll find that you look at things a little differently.

The more you travel, the more you become citizen of the world. We learn about other languages, traditions, food, cultures, and people. This helps us understand what tolerance and adaptability are and make us grow from many points of view. Our character and personality are still forming during our youth, so it turns out to be the perfect time to travel!

I have learned in my time abroad that people are generally very friendly and love to talk about their home and culture. This is not always the case, but it is more often. Making friendships abroad can make this big world seem a little smaller and help you feel more connected wherever you go.

The best advice I can give is to meet as many people on your travels as you can. It will make your time abroad more enjoyable since the locals know best! Plus, you never know when these connections will come in handy in the future, whether visiting each other for fun or otherwise.

Also, it has been believed that travelling increases self-confidence, facilitating interactions with people of the opposite sex. Talking about our travels also makes us appear fascinating and exciting, helping us cultivate interpersonal relationships.

The Science Behind It

Not only have I had the opportunity to do and see amazing things, but I've also met incredible people, I've travelled to eye-opening places, and I've had experiences that most people can only dream of. I know how lucky I am to have had the chance to travel as I have. Especially after visiting so many places and seeing people living with so little or nothing at all, I don't think I'll ever take what I have for granted. I don't think I'll ever want for anything, and many of the trivial things that may have mattered to me at one time wouldn't bother me as much anymore. I feel lucky to have gained this appreciation that I can carry with me for the rest of my life.

As per Contiki's research, a global travel company focusing on social travel for young travellers, travelling young provides incredible benefits.

In a sample size of 3,000 18–35-year-olds, Contiki's study found conclusive data revealing the long list of positive effects travel has on your teens. According to the survey, travel has a positive and lasting impact on young people's future careers, political involvement, and goal orientation.

Travelling makes us more productive and energetic. It is probably due to the relaxation of the holidays that allow you to recharge, the free mind, and the thoughts that remain at home. The statistics confirm this: in cities where workers have more vacation days, there is also greater productivity at work and professional level.

Travel seems to benefit young travellers' confidence, self-sufficiency, cultural awareness, acceptance, and adaptability. For those travelling internationally, their experiences positively impact their personal belief in themselves —paramount in a young adult's development. The more we travel, the more we want to do it again. It often happens in many other areas, but in this case, the "spirit of the traveller" lights up within us: the desire for freedom and discovery struggles with the search for a stable routine. The advantage of being young is that there is a time for stability, and therefore it is easier to choose to continue travelling. An older person, especially if he has a family, rightly lets responsibilities win and miss out on many emotions.

According to the study, 75 percent of young adults surveyed have a positive perception of themselves and their place in the world after travelling. Of course, having a positive experience while travelling will reverberate into our everyday lives.

Some other study findings explained how young travellers tend to be more outgoing and open-minded than young adults who do not have the opportunity to travel. By endeavouring on something new, whether a trip or job, having a positive experience can boost an individual's confidence.

According to the study, 42 percent of young travellers appear to have strong interpersonal connections and are more likely to seek new friendships, and feel more confident in new relationships. This makes them more successful in establishing a career, maintaining marketable skills, adapting to new situations, being creative, being successful in their careers, and meeting new challenges.

Being able to travel at a young age is a fantastic privilege that young adults benefit from. Whether travelling with your kids at a young age, hearing about their travel abroad programs or taking trips with them as adults, the benefits to travel go beyond just having a good time.

Some trips can change your life. We could go to a city, feel it is ours, and decide to move. Or we could meet a particular person. Therefore, it could turn out to be a one-way trip or the beginning of many trips to that specific half.

So if you are young and reading this, I implore you to travel and make your life an exciting story.

Actions to take before moving to the Next Chapter:

• If you are under 40 and want to taste what I just explained, I implore you to plan a Solo Trip and Book a Strictly Hostel for this trip. If it's terrifying, or if you are not sure, then even two days of a solo trip is fine as well. MAKE IT HAPPEN NOW!

• Make a personal blog or a diary or even a draft in your email where you jot down all your travel experiences even if it sounds ridiculous to do so. Trust me, when you grow old and recap all the exciting things you have done in the past, you tend to have hope in life and encouragement from your past. ONLY YOU CAN BE YOUR BEST MOTIVATOR!

CHAPTER THREE

The Power of Solo Travelling

You never really travel alone. The world is full of friends waiting to know you.

I have specially written this chapter because I get this question most of the time. Living in India, we tend to do things in social circles. Right from childhood, we are taught to have more friends, to have more people to play with, or just more people around to make us feel safe. This goes on with our lives to always have more people around us to feel safe and sane.

Look from Teenage to Adulthood, most of us stay with families very long, most of us go on holidays either with the extended part of our families or in groups with friends. This makes us comfortable with the thought that travelling is always about people and not about places. Even I agree on this to a certain point, but what we are missing here is that travel is also about YOU.

The individual in a travel equation is considered the lowest priority because our society has never been comfortable with this thought just enough. Our vacations are primarily focused on what places we would explore, what food we will get, how comfortable the hotel would be, how many ratings the hotel has, whether that location has enough charm for Instagram, and that place costs more than it should. These are the first questions we get when planning any vacation or travel. Instead, we should normalize asking the below questions.

Is the desired location good for me on a personal level? Do I feel to visit there because it would be an exploration of new territory, new culture? Can I promise myself to take this vacation as a break from routine life and not as another task? Can I plan it in a way that my package covers the most critical finance elements pre hand, so I do not have to make those decisions on the go? Can I make sure that I enjoy this break or vacation to recharge myself for a better routine coming ahead?

If you ask the later part of questions before any trip, Kudos! It's a way to go, proving that you take vacations considering a lot more information about you and your mental health. But if you are from a group that asks the first set of questions and not the second, then it's high time to change this mindset and focus on YOU.

There are endless reasons I could explain why you should travel solo at least once a year till you can because there is no experience like it.

Let us see why Solo Travel Actually makes a lot of sense sometimes.

Being Alone for a while is Healthy

Life is what we make of it.
Travels are travellers.
What we see is not what we see, but what we are.
(Fernando Pessoa, The book of restlessness)

Strange thing, isn't it? Why would you like to be lonely and consider this as a good thing coming out of a solo trip? You will get lonely travelling by yourself. Anyone who tells you differently is lying. But loneliness gets a bad rap. Let me explain!

Loneliness taught me how I like to spend my time. Understanding my own pace, rhythms, and preferences has impacted every corner of my life, including where and how I live. We so rarely have time to be still, to be with ourselves. Travelling solo gives that gift.

It takes practice, being alone. Here are a few tips that helped me:

1. Resist the urge to be busy all the time. Don't fill every waking moment. Let yourself be. Loneliness isn't boredom.

2. Don't keep in touch. I have a difficult time being in the moment, and I miss loved ones more if I keep in close contact while I'm away (including posting on and checking social media). I've conditioned my friends and family that no news is good news. They know my itinerary, and I check in regularly and briefly, but stories and pictures can wait until I get home.

3. Your demons will follow you. You can't outrun them. So, turn around, face them, and invite them to have a cup of tea with you. By now, I'm old friends with mine.

4. On travels, you find yourself when you are alone, in different corners, along forgotten roads. When you are yourself, you always find life.

5. Arriving at each new city, the traveller rediscovers a past that he no longer knew he had: the strangeness of what you're no longer or no longer possess awaits you at the crossing in foreign and un-owned places.

6. The journey never ends. Only travellers end up. And they too can be prolonged in memory, in remembrance, in

narration. When the traveller sat down on the sand of the beach and said: "There is nothing else to see," he knew it was not true. We must see what we have not seen, see again what we have already seen, see in spring what we have seen in summer, see during the day what we have seen at night, with the sun where it rained the first time, see the green crops, the ripe fruit, the stone that changed its place, the shadow that wasn't there. It is necessary to return to the steps already given, repeat them, and trace new paths alongside them. We have to start the journey again.

7. Travelling is when you organize a destination and make an unexpected one; travelling is knowing by which means to go and not by which to return; travelling means being satisfied regardless of the outcome of the trip; travelling is feeling free from all stereotypes and catalysts; travelling is knowing that you are one, no one, but a solo traveller to trace new paths.

Making Friends around the world is cool

The only real journey, the only bath of youth, would not be to go towards new landscapes but to have different eyes, to see the universe with the eyes of another, of a hundred others, to see a hundred galaxies that each of us they see, that each of them is.

When you travel solo, you end up meeting many amazing people out there who are doing crazy things you could only imagine. You meet people from all ages, all walks of life, and there is no shortage of college students' inspiration to people in old age travelling the world.

Also, think of the networking and help you can get from having friends worldwide. Let me share my personal experience.

I met 陳智捷 (English Name: James) in a hostel in Paris, as he was there to learn cooking and we became friends really quick as he was super friendly and drinks beer :P

After having great conversations over a couple of days in a hostel, I became interested in his country, i.e., Taiwan, as he started telling me a lot about it, and trust me, I was sold.

Almost after a year, I got the opportunity to plan Taiwan but was a bit nervous as it was an unknown non-English speaking territory for me.

However, it couldn't have been the best time to visit because James had come back to Taiwan from Paris and was in town. He helped me by answering all my questions over the chat, and we decided to meet once I was in Taiwan.

So finally, when he met me, surprisingly, he came with his best friend Michael Lin who was interested in meeting me, just out of curiosity to meet an English-speaking foreigner of his friend and also because he can practice English with me. He was really a super fun guy to be with!

That evening, they not only showed me around local/ meat markets, but they also gave me a ton of exciting information about a lot of its culture/tourism/regional history. They also helped me to try the best local bubble tea, a remarkable thing in Taiwan.

An interesting lesson I learned on that trip was that sometimes keeping in touch with people you met on your travel journey can make your future travel more accessible and make you feel at home in the countries you have never been to before.

I am very fortunate to have friends worldwide, even from the countries I have never been to(yet), and I am sure that I would feel very comfortable taking trips there because now I know I have someone already to make me feel at home anywhere I go.

You get a Management Degree to Tackle Anything

We all know how much things need to be coordinated before taking an extended vacation, let alone solo travelling. On the other hand, Solo travelling needs way more management than standard group tours. You have to do everything on your own, from your Visa if it's international travel to transportation to hostels to last-minute glitches.

It might sound like it's not worth going through such a mess if it's so hard, but remember, when you do all this management by yourself, you become a better person; you become a responsible person, not by choice but by circumstances. It is one of the best teachings you can ever take from travelling solo at the end of the day.

Also, there comes a time when you have to take care of your finances by not overspending on anything you like because there is no one to stop you, which indirectly makes you your own master, which can be a two-sided sword. If you spend more, you won't likely cover everything you wanted, and if you don't spend at all, you will feel like missing out, so you will have to manage the balance and prioritize what can be done and what can be skipped, which will never happen if you travel will group or someone else.

There are a lot of other things you learn. I remember when I took a solo trip to Europe, my first stop was a hotel in Paris, and for some reason, my bag lock was stuck when I tried to open it after settling on a bed in the 16-bed dorm room. The bag wasn't opening to my surprise and shock, and I had all my stuff in it.

Was I on a group tour, things would have been easy because someone would know someone and there would be help to get this solved quickly, but as I was travelling solo and it was my first day in Paris with my bag locked, I had no other option but to ask around from staff of hostel and search online. To my rescue, the hostel staff after suggesting many different options handed me an experimental type of scissors that could open almost anything, and after a trial error of around 45 mins, I broke my bag's lock to make it open.

These experiences feel challenging when you have them, but later, you eventually realize that any problem that comes in ahead of you, you will somehow manage it. And if this is not what a management degree should be, I don't know what is.

You can do Embarrassing things without being embarrassed

Let's admit that we always want to do silly things even when we are grown up, and it becomes hard to do that if you are travelling with someone else or in a group. We always want to visit the children's park and maybe have some rides which are made for kids, yet we don't do that in embarrassment. But guess what? If you travel solo, you can do anything you desire, even if it's stilly or embarrassing. There are no judgments, and even if there are judgments from strangers, the good news is you won't see them ever again.

When I was in Denmark, I came across this fantastic adventure park, and I did all the rides, even those with almost no adults on them. All the kids were looking at me with strange eyes, but as I said, I could do all the things I wanted as long as they were legal.

Feeling of Abundance

When we are running in our life doing our jobs and managing businesses, we tend to stop thinking anything beyond it, or we feel that magic or miracles happen only with others and not with us. But, when you travel solo, you understand how amazing the world can be with so many different opportunities. The primary reason for this is that you meet terrific people doing extraordinary things.

When you travel solo, you observe way more because you are out there just seeing and experiencing things on your own, and when you observe new things, you learn how tiny the place we occupy in this world and how small our issues are. This feeling is such a magic inside you, and you feel that there is no end to anything. The world has everything in abundance; it was just your view which was small or limited.

So in all senses, I implore you one more time to take the solo trip you have always been dreaming of because, at the end of the day, Solo travel makes more sense than many things, and it's always worth it!

How to Decide the destination for your solo trip?

You may wonder how people decide where to go next or what would be a fun location for solo travel, as you are the only one who should be excited about the destination you want to travel and explore.

More than one in two young people look for travel photos and holiday-themed posts on social media and say they are amused in doing so, while 40% of them use Instagram. They would even be places of unparalleled inspiration with hashtags — also very generic — such as #travel or #travel used to discover popular destinations and new destinations. It is a habit that the young generation seems to share with the immediate previous generation: even among Millennials, there are, in fact, 30% of travellers who base their travel choices on trends discovered on Instagram or who choose the destinations of their holidays according to how much they are instagrammable.

Women more than men — the percentage would, in fact, rise, in this case, to 47% — would be inclined to seek inspiration for travel on social media, as they do for purchases and consumption in other very different fields, from food to fashion.

When it comes to a consensus, however, influencers also seem to play their part: despite any prediction that influencer marketing wants in crisis, 45% of the booking.com sample admits to following travel influencers and travel bloggers to be inspired by destinations and destinations that they propose on their social profiles or blogs and, in 35% of cases to follow recommendations and advice regarding attractions to visit, places to eat and drink, hospitality.

This does not mean that very young give up completely the advice and recommendations of friends, family, acquaintances, and more generally of people who attend offline: for over 30% of the survey participants in question, in fact, the latter still plays a fundamental role.

However, an interesting fact concerns the inspiration that comes from cinema and TV series: one in three young people would choose for their holiday's famous places on the small and big screen, where they were filmed or that were the setting for the most loved cinema and television cult. A confirmation, the latest in chronological order that film tourism is an expanding sector, and that lives in very different declination, from the tour on the Game of Thrones sets to the trips to discover the closed area of Chernobyl, which became popular later the success of the homonymous series, passing through the possibility of sleeping in the desert house of the last season of Black Mirror.

Action Items before you move to the next chapter:

• Jot down a one or two-day solo trip if you are a beginner and plan all your details out and stick it somewhere where you can see that plan frequently

• Jot down things that you always wanted to do on a vacation, but you are afraid to do maybe because it's not your age to do those or if it's embarrassing and before taking a solo trip, make sure you find those places where you can do all these things

CHAPTER FOUR

PEOPLE ARE CONVERSATIONS

Have you been in a situation where you tried to replace someone by doing the same thing with a different person, but you failed? Well, we all have! But what do you get as a result? No satisfaction, and do you wonder why?

Because people are conversations, people are defined by how they make conversations, what they talk, how they gloriously explain their dreams, how they put their point in front of you, and how they respect your thoughts even if they don't align well. Everything above makes us who we are.

I know there is a lot more in a person than conversation like their personality, clothing, style, which makes them who they are, but if you think of it, at the end of the day, with what do you fall? Is it just clothes, style, cars, money, or conversations? Because simply whatever a person is, the only way to know more about him is by knowing his thoughts turned into words.

Perhaps, the conversation is not just random talking. It is a lot more than that because talking can be done with anyone, but why don't you like everyone? Because conversation is an art that not everyone possesses, which makes us be more with those who have mastered this art. Else, why would you pay huge money to be with counsellors, motivators, and shrinks if they didn't have art to make you listen to them and influence your thoughts and actions?

A considerable part of any successful person is what they speak and with whom because conversations can change your thoughts, impact your actions and lead to different results in your life. You might have heard that person A was a failure, but after getting a mentor, the same person became successful; no doubt the actions were changed, but what changed them? Right Conversations with Right People!! In our lives, we have often been able to pass through our most challenging times because there were correct conversations in our lives, making us think towards optimistic hopes!

Also, have you wondered why we explore people even when they have the same human body/status/culture? Because we crave variety, and hunger for variety never dies, which gets satisfied only when you listen to different kinds of conversations in the form of thoughts/ experiences, which probably makes life very interesting for most of us!

Most of us are usually defined by mass conversations or thoughts around us, which is the basic foundation of any religion/cult/culture and even community. Because conversations are not random talks but talks with the intention of something, if I am a salesperson, my conversation would consistently lead to selling you something or telling you how great it would be if you buy from me. Similarly, the conversation is a talk with intent.

When it comes to travelling the world, you cannot imagine the variety of people you get and the variety of conversations you can indulge in. If you travel to a part of a world that is not yet developed or there are still significant issues, you will find your conversations very different with local people. The talks would be more about how they face poverty, how governments are not listening to them, how poor medical care is in the country, or how bad it is to expect basic things like clean water, good food, etc.

Similarly, if you travel to a part of the world where the advances are significant, you would indulge mostly in conversations about how they are trying to reduce the carbon footprint, how they are trying to build machines that would do better work than humans, how they are making policies where medical care becomes much better.

Now, if you observe just two paragraphs above, you will get an idea of how different conversations could take place in other parts of the world and just imagine how much you would grow as a person if you can indulge in totally different conversations at different places with different people. All it takes is that you travel and connect with different people, especially locals of any area.

Let me share some more reasons why people are conversations:

Everyone is unique and so are conversations

I believe the world is full of magic because we don't even know what we don't know and that gives us great hope of learning something and being amazed about it. So, when you talk with different people, you know exciting things from very different walks of life.

In 2018, I quit my high-paying job and took a gap year to travel the world and stay in hostels and meet new people. Given the country I live in, India, it was way too big a deal, and a weird step given the upbringing we have that young age is just for earning good so that you can have a better life in future. Because of this, I faced many challenges starting from meeting my friends to visa consulates. Everyone was either shocked or thought I am crazy to do that.

However, fast forward to Istanbul, Turkey. I met this guy in a hostel from Kazakhstan, and we shared a couple of dinners and went around the market a few times, and to my shock, I came to know he has been travelling for five years. Five freaking years!

He shared such different and incredible stories that I started to laugh at my fear of taking just a 1-year gap. This is what conversations do to you. They shape you into something which you cannot do or struggle to do by yourself.

This is why when you meet different people, you have unique conversations that literally break your mind and give you new thoughts you never expected.

Everyone has a different upbringing

The beauty of the world is that everyone has a different upbringing. We all are brought up in very different religions, financial statuses, philosophies, let alone different continents or countries. This makes us very unique from the point of perception. Two people coming from different upbringings will see the same thing in a completely different way. That may be exactly the same, or they may be totally opposite of each other. This makes us different and different people create different conversations.

When we come from a different part of the land, we come with very different perspectives. I was in Australia, and it was my first country, so I was very observant of even small things. In some of the restaurants, they had pictures of African Starving kids near dustbins, and it said, "The Food waste we create can finish the hunger of 100 kids every day." I instantly felt that many things we do in our countries are very normal and even trendy, like ordering extra than you actually need or just throwing delicious food into a bin because it had a bit more pepper. Still, the same thing in other parts of the world would be a disaster.

The same food we waste could be a life-saving meal for someone somewhere around the world. So when you talk with different people who come from other upbringings/ foreign land, you realize that something normal for you could be a huge deal for someone else. This creates a tremendous sense of humility and whatever you do when you go back to your comfort zone.

Everyone has a different style of sharing

This is a critical reason we love to listen to different people and get influenced by them. If you listen to Gary V or Tony Robbins or anyone, you will find that you crave their content. Why is that? Is it because they say something which has never been said before? Is it because they are from the future? NO!

It's because everyone shares knowledge or facts in different styles and manners, giving us new perceptions even from the same old philosophies. You would notice that sometimes the same thing you have heard from your friends or parents often starts making sense if someone explained it to you differently. Because every person has a different tone, facial expression, and way of telling things, some people are great influencers, and some people are never heard even when they have a great wealth of knowledge to share.

Some people tell stories in a way that feels like everything is fiction, and some people tell you things in a way that you think wrong about everything. There are so many different ways to share anything, but the style of doing it makes a huge difference. That's why conversations are like storytelling, and when you get great storytellers, you enjoy the time and learn a lot at the same time.

World is changing and so are people!

Imagine talking about travel in the 1990s and now Imagine talking about the trip in 2022! Every part of the conversation would be different. Not only travel but related to anything. The reason is that the world is changing at an incredible speed and so are people's views. Observe the kids these days. The kids of the 1990s used to go out and play or eat dirt and enjoy outdoor activities, and today, kids enjoy iPad and do not eat unless they watch cartoons on TV or YouTube. The world has changed a lot, and it will always keep changing.

When it comes to travel, it changes a lot of factors to discuss. The people before this generation used to discuss things in their country, and it was beyond our wildest imagination. Now, people tell you via Images and articles that give us more significant insights and instant access to see images, videos, and commentary without even visiting the place.

Similarly, with the changing world, the people are changing. People worldwide now use the internet to make travel plans; they use various kinds of different websites to know more about minute things that were impossible before.

So, when we meet people in today's era, it's not that they are unaware of things that were supposed to be shocking 100 years back. Because of Instagram, overexposure to the internet and technology, somewhere, people have heard some exciting things about your country already.

Everyone has a story

The magical thing about this world is that it's crazy! Don't get me wrong. I meant in a perfect way. The world is filled with eight billion+ people, millions of different species, and trillions of things we have made. It is one crazy phenomenon. With this much craziness, it is so easy to find unique people and unique stories if we look at it.

Trust me; I have met so many crazy people worldwide who have built a belief system inside me that the world is a fantastic place. You will find that everyone has their own story with many differences in languages, culture, countries, rules, and religions. There might be certain elements common between some groups, but at the end of the day, you will never find two people having the exact same life.

This reason itself should motivate you to travel the world and meet as many different people as possible. Because when you learn about others' stories, you realize that everyone has a story that is so different from what you have ever heard before.

To give you a glimpse, I have met people who have been travelling solo for five years and do not even know when they are going back home; I have met people who go to the airport and then decide where to travel in the world. I have met a 16-year-old girl who was pregnant and was in discussion with her family and her boyfriend to plan the life for the child. I have just met so many people that have led me to believe that everyone has a great story and if you put an effort to listen, to know about it, you will know wonders!

The best part of travelling is that you get ample opportunities to search these conversations. You never know where you meet random people and see a bit about their life and learn something totally new.

How to overcome self-doubt conversations in your head!

When you take the step to travel, you are about to leave for unknown lands where your life will change in such a drastic way that it will be incomprehensible to you. How can you even imagine what awaits you?

Your normal life will change forever, and even if the thrill of what lies ahead is intense, some doubts will buzz in your head.

'What if I can't do it?' 'What if life on the road isn't for me?' 'How the heck am I going to talk to people in languages, I don't know?'

And perhaps the greatest of fears ... 'What happens if I don't speak to anyone at all?'

But trust me, you will be creating deep bonds while travelling, which is so rewarding in itself. Maybe it's because you are the most vulnerable version of yourself.

There are no friends to shield you, no familiar bars or familiar places, and a whole new language to deal with. When you create a relationship, you do it solely thanks to yourself in your most natural form!

Travelling could, in theory, be the loneliest thing to do because you keep moving and cannot create lasting relationships. But this is not true; the relationships you will create while travelling will be strong.

There are interesting people behind every door, in every bar, on every beach, and on every mountain climb. Smile, be open, listen, observe, and ask questions. It does not matter if you are under the covers in your bed in the hostel or if you are pushing yourself to conquer the Inca Trail: there are interesting people everywhere.

And guess what, you are interesting too! Even if you've always lived in a city, town, or village, no one has ever heard of it. Maybe so far, your life has revolved around school, university, or work. It does not matter!

Travelling allows you to strip yourself of your 'polluted' layers. Your past, your problems, complicated relationships, and any embarrassing situations you have become attached to will begin to seem less important to you.

People's impressions will no longer control you; the baggage you carried with you in everyday life will disappear as you wander around in anonymity, ready to enjoy your conversations with all.

Far from your community, from your group, from your old friends, you will find yourself. You may feel a little lost; perhaps you will find yourself timidly watching on the sidelines. Or you will go straight to the closest group that reminds you of friends back home. And then, as you become more confident, you will gravitate toward what you don't know.

Give yourself time to let go of everything you thought you were, and continue to strip yourself of your layers until you are nothing but the essence of yourself.

Action Items before you move to the next chapter:

• Assess and jot down some of the unique things you like about your best friend or partner and what thought process makes them special enough. Embrace that and, if possible, also appreciate them about this explicitly!

• Assess and write down which types of books/movies or motivational speakers you like and why? What is something you specifically like about them?

CHAPTER FIVE

How to Travel for Almost Free!

It sounds absurd, right? That you don't need much money to travel or you can travel for free. But you read it right. To travel the world, you don't need a massive amount of money; instead, you need a tremendous amount of courage and creativity with a crazy passion for exploring the world.

But even then, you would think it takes a lot of money to travel. Well, not always! In this section, I'll explain how to save while travelling, or better still, "how to travel for free or almost"! Don't you believe it? You will be amazed at how many systems there are.

We live in the most incredible time ever with so much technology around us everywhere. There are things now possible that would be impossible even to think of some years back. Being said this, we have opportunities around us to do what we want at a minimal cost, more than we could ever do it before.

In a moment, we will discuss all factors, from travelling for free to having a free stay. Still, before that, I would like you to focus that this chapter is not about telling you that travelling can be done for free, but rather this chapter is about telling you that there are a lot of ways where you can travel for a low price if you use the creative options, we have all around us.

Before we break it down into technical elements and go through it, I want you to understand that it's more about mindset than about reality. There are off course, different types of people when it comes to travel. Some want to explore the world, however much struggle it is. Some people like to stay only in 5-star hotels and see the only sophisticated part of the world; some people love to be involved so much in a culture that they never stay in hotels instead find local homestays.

The world is filled with different travellers, and there is no end to how different people want to enjoy travelling differently.

Now let's break it down to some ninja techniques to use less money and more creativity.

Flights

The flights to any place are undoubtedly our most significant expense if we travel anywhere on budget, especially if it's very far from where you live. Sometimes the prices are shocking and make no sense, and sometimes the prices are meager but with some restrictions such as non-refundable/nonflexible/no luggage, etc.

If your trip requires a flight, you must play cunningly to save money. In the meantime, follow the airlines on social media, subscribe to the newsletters, monitor any special offers; you may find the right offer for you. Or maybe you might come across tickets for a low price and, depending on that, choose the destination.

With a massive increase in travel, the airline industry has adjusted to having dynamic pricing structures that serve them well. They can increase or decrease the price by the minute as per demand and supply rather than keeping a fixed price. This can be disheartening, but it also opens up many different opportunities to get a great bargain if you put some effort into strategies.

Let's dive in to explore options that can help you cut this cost and maybe even get free flights.

Hack 1: Credit Cards

Credit cards are fantastic if you use them wisely and pay your bills in full every month. If you don't, then skip this option.

If you travel a lot or tend to do so, or want to avail travel benefits on the go, you can always sign up with Co-branded Credit Cards, which will help you earn points with every credit card transaction. These days, almost every big travel company has its own co-branded credit cards, which can be redeemed on flights/hotels after a certain threshold. Even if you do not plan to have co-branded cards, these days, most of the credit card companies let you redeem your reward points against flights. So, the key to getting the most out of a credit card is to use the same card for all the transactions, so the rewards points keep accumulating.

Whichever country you are located in, just a simple google search as 'Travel Branded Credit Cards' will bring up a list of the most famous credit card options available, which will help you convert its point into miles and can be redeemed against flight tickets.

Hack 2: Make use of Deals Websites

If you want to get the best deals, there are many great websites to create alerts and keep yourself informed with the best deals happening on your route. If you want to have an example, you can check Skyscanner.com to get the best flight deals possible from various websites in one place. Also, you can create alerts to get an email as soon as you get the flights in the price range you want. As I said before, dynamic airline policies have both pros and cons, and as a traveller, you always have to try to use them for your own benefit.

Subscribe to travel agency websites to get the latest deals, especially if you plan to travel frequently, so you not only get updates, but you can mix and match things from different sources to save vast amounts on flights.

If you are travelling solo, you should check out budget airlines. They have special cheap rates for most of the places. The only restriction they usually have is luggage. They allow 6-7kg, but it cannot get any better if you are young and not very clingy.

If, on the other hand, you are sufficiently organized by destination and departure period, browse the comparison engines incognito. I suggest Skyscanner, Flyforfree, lastminute.com.

Remember: It is better to book the round trip separately and with different companies. You could take advantage of two special travel offers. On the contrary, do not be seduced by excessively low prices for the outbound flight coupled with exorbitant return tickets.

Stay

Once you have taken care of travel arrangements, the next big thing to plan for anyone is to stay. Some places can be costly to stay. Europe/Canada or most first-world countries can sometimes cost you $50 or more per night. It also happens with many people who get cheap flight offers, but the cost of stay is very high, and the plan has to be dropped. But if you read this further, you will know how you can live anywhere in the world for almost free.

Accommodation is likely to be the saltiest part of your trip. But even here, you can find a solution for free or almost. Of course, you have to forget about the existence of hotels, B & Bs and the like. Instead, be prepared to stay in other people's homes. Do you know, for example, Home Exchange? People from different countries travel around the world and exchange the homes for a period of time. Checkout the movie called 'The Holiday' and also checkout the website called https://www.homeexchange.com/

Sounds absurd again? Well, It's a fact, and millions of people do this every year. Let's dig more options.

Hack 1 : CouchSurfing

Couch Surfing (https://www.couchsurfing.com) is not just a website, but basically, a community where you can request people to stay at their home for absolutely free! You would ask, what's the catch? The answer is 'There is no Catch.' Couch Surfing is a community of travellers and like-minded people who help each other by providing free stay/ sometimes free food. In exchange, you write a review about your visit, and this way, the profile gets built up. So, for example, if I have helped ten people from different countries to stay at my place for free and have great reviews, in return I can ask for a free stay whenever I am travelling next, and with the great reviews, I can get a free stay, and this goes on. Technology has given us things that were impossible a few years back.

You will ask yourself: why do I have to go to sleep at someone else's house? Overcome the embarrassment and think instead that meeting someone local will help you immerse yourself in the local context. The person who will host you can be a good help and reference for you throughout the journey.

And if you want a minimum of privacy without going to a hotel, I recommend camping: a sleeping bag, backpack, and instructions for setting up a tent. However, you will need to find out about places to sleep first if you don't want to incur fines and problems with the local authorities.

Hack 2: Exchange your skills for Free Stay and Free Food

If you can do anything, you can stay for free. If you know any other language, computer, or any skill or know-how to put bed sheet and clean toilet, you can stay for free.

Many portals let you find hostels or hosts that would need your 4 hours per day; in exchange, they give you a free bed and free meals. You can also have work flexibility and maybe work just mornings or just afternoons, and the rest of the day is yours to explore. If this idea pleases you, you can check https://www.workaway.info or https://www.helpstay.com and get yourself registered there.

Usually, the hostels require you for a week minimum to a couple of months. You can always check host details before sending them your profile for approval. This helps hostels cut down expenses on hiring people for work that anyone can do and make hostels multicultural.

I have met many people in hostels who are doing bartending, cleaning, the receptionist who are not locals, but travellers exchanging skills for a free stay and free meals. Some hostels also provide you with more benefits like free tours, vouchers, etc.

Hack 3: Facebook Groups/Social Media

Though social media is a web where you cannot trust someone blindly, if you are friends with someone or are involved in a travel community, you can always ask help for accommodation in the groups themselves. I have seen many people getting great hosts who are not on Airbnb or any other website but are ready to host people free from the trusted groups or community.

Personally, before going anywhere, I join a lot of groups of that country and try to make local friends and more than often, I get great people who are ready to host me for free or at least help me to find some of the cheapest accommodations which do not make it to the internet.

Today, social media is no longer just a place to see what your friends are doing or what companies have to offer you. It has become a place where you can build authentic connections, take real profits from groups of like-minded people, or even get yourself a place for free. If you are creative about this, you can find a place to stay for free anywhere you go.

Tours & Attractions

If your travel arrangements and stay are sorted, you might ask what to do about tours? How do you get them for free, or is it even possible? The answer is YES! You can get free tours.

When you stay in a hostel, there are many tours arranged for tourists, which are free and tip-based. You can tip whatever you feel is suitable for the tour. You can pay from $1 to $100, whatever you think it's worth, and as per your budget.

Even if you are not staying in a hostel and are staying anywhere else, you can Google local walking tours, and you will get many links/google listings with locations and timetables. Or you can call any hostel nearby and ask for free walking tours, and they will be happy to help you even if you are not staying with them as the tour is tip-based anyway.

These walking tours are excellent. You get to choose from many different theme-based walking tours. Some are based on historical themes, some are based on showing you the most famous sites, and most are mixed. So once you decide which free tour you want to do, you need to reach the starting point at a designated time, and you will meet the guide at that spot. They explain to you about the tour and then take you on a free walking tour for around 1-3 hours depending on the country, weather, theme, etc.

At the end of the tour, they ask you for the tip which you think is worth the tour and depending on your budget and liking of the tour; you can pay at the end of the tour. You often make really cool friends on walking tours who are also on a budget or want to explore more, keeping other factors in mind.

Apart from free walking tours and free attractions in the country, some websites can help you get the unbelievable cheapest deals only if you know the correct timing to look for bargains.

Some of the best portals for great deals are: Groupon (Respective country will have respective URL), another one is Klook (https://klook.com/), and you can be creative and find more websites with terms as 'Local Travel Deals' for the country you want better deals. With the help of portals like these, I have saved thousands of bucks already.

Food

Usually, if you use any of the above hacks, you get free food in exchange for your skills or sometimes even in your couch surfing stay. However, there are other ways out there.

Hack 1 : Use Yelp or Foursquare

Many new restaurants/cafes worldwide want excellent reviews from real users. The best way is to offer something free and ask for a review/check-in. You can find the locals on these apps and try looking at their offers. Usually, they provide free Slice of Pizza or Buy One/Get One free offer, but sometimes some cafes offer full meals. It depends on your luck and location.

If the food is not free, worry about shopping yourself in an ordinary supermarket. If you want to eat out, choose street food. You will find that it will give you back the dimension of the local culture in addition to costing less.

Hack 2: Find Coupons

There are many local magazines/newspapers in hostels or on subways with a couple of great deals for local cafes and restaurants, which can be handy for budget food or for redeeming nice offers.

Another way which is good if you are a religious person is to visit Gurudrawa for Langer (Food), which is served every day for free without any conditions. This might be the best idea if you are interested in tasting different food.

Hack 3: Save even before leaving

As little as you may spend on travel, never think about leaving with less money.

We hope that everything goes well, but keep in mind that in case of unforeseen events, you should be able to open your wallet and, above all, be able to find the money inside!

Before concluding, I want to remind you to save money for travelling and create a small capital that will make you live your trip in peace.

Free Visas

Visa is permission to enter the country, and the rules are crazy. So I can share generic experiences and tricks, but it largely depends on where you stay.

For Indians, Visa-free countries are limited. However, those countries can still be explored really well without spending a bomb amount of money on Visa Fees and harassment by providing a pile of documents to prove you do not have bad intentions.

Some beautiful countries do not require any visa costs for Indians, like Indonesia, Mauritius, etc. All you need is a confirmed stay and some money to show to immigration. Rules keep changing from time to time, so it's always better to check out official immigration information before planning.

It's More About Mindset Than Actual Spending

The above tricks and hacks work best only if you are not behind saving JUST money and do not plan to enjoy your travel. It might sound ironic to read this after reading about saving tricks.

Due to my travel experience, I have helped many people plan many trips and have shared these things, but as I have said before, these are hacks, and sometimes they work, sometimes they don't. So, if you keep a rigid mindset and get disheartened if this doesn't work, I would suggest to not even try and plan your travel only if you have a reasonable budget.

But if you travel intending to travel and try these hacks, results would be more fruitful. So I implore you to travel the world and find your own creative ways to make a perfect balance between your expenses and travel experiences.

Action Items before you move to the next chapter:

• Once you have decided the destination to travel, find the local websites which offers the travel deals

• Visit Viator, Klook, Groupon and check out the prices for those specific activities on all these websites.

• Check the Facebook groups for that country/location and connect with few local people to get the deals/contact numbers which do not make it to the internet.

• YouTube the country/location and check if you can find creative ways of saving money using other's experience

Happy Travel Hacking!!

CHAPTER SIX

Why Journey is More Important than a Destination?

Just reaching a destination doesn't matter at all!

Let's see an example clearly depicting this:

Suppose you are embarking on a journey to your favourite place, let's say Kashmir; after all, it's our very own Indian Paradise.

- **Case A:** You eventually reach Kashmir, but your experience may be unwanted life thrills, be it stone-pelting, or with unfortunate and doomed tiring incidents like a puncture in a tire of your bus or maybe someone falling ill happening along the way. In this case, you would have not really enjoyed your trip but left with all the bittersweet memories.

- **Case B:** You enjoyed singing, dancing, and playing throughout the journey, enjoying the beautiful sceneries of the valley, and then reached Kashmir. And hence, indeed, the nature of the journey and how well did you enjoy it decide the whole trip's pleasure.

Many people do not believe in enjoying the journey and hope a beautiful destination makes everything worth it. Still, those are the same people who constantly live life in a result-oriented way and be happy only when they see results in personal and professional life! And we all know how those people behave while being on the journey or being in the process.

What the destination actually is, matters relatively very less!

The place where you go has less importance than the company you have had, the experiences you have gained, and the memories you have made. Sure, the place is proud to boast it off, but the smiles and the inner feeling are even more priceless.

Whether we go to North or South, be in Swadesh or Videsh when we have crazy companions whom we can enjoy with, what difference does it make, isn't it? While it may matter in aspects of what all activities you do.

For example, You would only be able to enjoy skiing at places with snowy landscapes, Rafting only riverside places, or experience relaxing calmness at places free of the hustle and bustle.

But imagine what if you choose the best place, but the climate changes all of a sudden, or you reach there and see either too much snow or too little that could destroy your travel plan.

Thus, most of the time, the destination is trivial to what you feel and enjoy about your journey.

Always a chance for the unplanned adventure!

Every trip majorly depends on many factors like health, mood, and other situations. Dependents like immediate ones like the people you're travelling with or indirect ones like travel guides or bookings made, etc.

Sometimes also on bad weather or climatic conditions, a natural disaster, etc., or perhaps situations like wallet theft or losing any of your valuable things, train/ booking cancellations.

And all of these factors are pretty out of our hands to control. So, quick amendments are required for your plans as the situation demands. It's all about those little things and pleasures which make any tour memorable!

It's not just about the tour but also the surviving skills in constant use. Also, the goof-ups we make during and around the tour that decides its overall experience!

Things as small as the conversations we made with others which could deepen our relationship further or finding broader perspectives of life by self-analysis along with experiencing the breezy air from the window, new local food, crazy photos, etc., are the things that you take with you after a trip forever...

And to take away all the sweet memories, all you need to do is be present at the moment, forget all your worries and live it to the fullest, which can only be done if you enjoy the journey as equally as you enjoy your destination!

Journey when compared to Life

Metaphorically, it still holds the same relevance when we link this idea to life. Destinations are indeed mirages; they don't exist, and we continuously keep redefining them as per the interests we develop now and then.

Many times, in life, we chase a destination and then stop or change it in the middle. Still, we learn various new things along the way, and this learning and re-iterating of definitions of our destinations are more important than reaching the destination itself.

So, even though we don't always reach them, we could always accomplish things we wished for, like happiness, which were the ultimate goals to have destinations in the first place. They sure are suitable for setting a direction to our journeys initially, but with time all that matters is how we spend most of the time, first handily experiencing everything in life.

"Indeed, Journey is more important, and so is creating memories!"

So, whether it's 'Life' or 'Travel,' make sure you enjoy your journey because that's what really counts!

Journey Teaches you lessons destination cannot teach

When you travel the world or even anywhere unknown, you face things that you might have never encountered before in life. But if you come to think of it, your hotel room is pretty much the same in every city in the world.

While going through a journey, you learn a lot about dependency, learning to trust strangers, and learning many trivial things that would make you a different person altogether. There are many things that happen to you on a journey, be it good or bad. Be it travel or life. The journey teaches you far more things than your destination ever will.

Journey makes your failure seems okay

You know how our plans turn out to be different from what actually happens in reality. We plan everything perfectly; we sometimes overthink and over plan even small things, like planning exact routes, ways, etc. But when you really go for it, sometimes things are very different.

If happiness is a goal for you, what if it doesn't come?

Let's say you have a goal, which represents happiness; if this goal is not achieved, what would happen? In addition to losing the beauty of what happens around that goal, you will experience a profound sense of defeat, and you will feel surrounded by misery.

The goal of happiness takes away the focus from the present.

If you always think that you will be happy when something ends when a negative period has passed, or at the end of the year, you find yourself chasing happiness that you will not see, and in the meantime, you will have missed all the positives that life was giving you. This moment, even if it seems like the wrong time. Try to focus on what you have rather than what you don't have, and seek happiness in the present.

The Paris Incident

I remember my incident when I was backpacking solo in Europe. I wanted to plan everything ahead of time. I even planned routes from bus stops to hostels and vice versa.

As I usually hopped between countries via busses, this time I had planned to travel to Berlin from Paris by Bus, and as per my plan, I thought it would take a max of 30mins in a taxi from my hostel to the Bus stop. When I took a cab, the cab driver did not speak even one word of English, and that worried me a bit, but as you know, we live in an advanced world, and we mostly rely on technology, so I was okay as he was using his GPS to get me to the bus stop.

Near the bus stop, around 10 PM in Paris, the guy could not understand where to go, and he started speaking French with me. I had no idea what was happening, so I figured that he might have a problem understanding the road because the GPS showed a road that we could not see. After turning two rounds on the same street, the guy stops in the middle of nowhere and speaks French with a body language that I am stopping the ride here, and you are on your own.

I was so scared because I did not understand a word he said, and I could miss my bus due to that, and it would be a disaster to replan everything and lose money on my hostels.

I got down from my Taxi and started seeking help from people/bus drivers, anyone I could see, and when I almost gave up, one truck driver spoke a little bit of English and got my problem solved. He then explained to the driver that the road is a tunnel displayed on the map and hence you can't clearly see it visually, and It would be best if you took a specific street to hit that road.

When I finally reached the bus stop, I missed my bus, and there was no bus for another few hours until 4 AM. Disheartened, hungry, and alone, I just sat there and started to smile. Not because I am crazy, but because I realized that whatever you plan, however perfect you plan, there will always be something you would not be prepared for. There would always be that 'X' element that you can never think of unless it happens.

Since then, I have always been prepared to be okay with failures, missing buses, flights, or sometimes failing on the perfect plans I made because, just like life, we cannot plan journeys. The journey is all about experiencing the flow, which might always be in ups and downs, but that makes it more of a learning instrument and magical. Wouldn't you agree?

Journey Builds Character

Do you know the set-point theory of happiness? According to this theory, your level of well-being is determined by characteristic traits rooted in your personality. Based on this theory, regardless of what happens in your life, you will have a constant level of happiness without feeling the ups and downs intensely. This theory supports the view of happiness as a journey and not as an endpoint.

Believe it or not. Be it life or travelling, what you do in your journey towards your destination says a lot about your character. What you do on your trip means how you behave in unknown situations. When you travel, especially solo, there are many many situations that you might have never experienced before and would have never been ready for it.

Be it immigration, be it airports, be it a hostel, be it anything unknown to you, your character or ethics come out when you are on your own in a situation where your action changes consequences. When you travel solo, you do not always meet amazing people in hostels or amazing customs officers. Sometimes you meet people with unexplainable agendas, and you won't even understand what is going on due to cultural differences.

I remember my experience when I travelled solo to Macau, which is very rare, especially being Indian. People from all over the world visit Macau primarily for Gambling as it's the Las Vegas of Asia. As soon as I landed from my flight and went towards immigration, around four customs officers surrounded me and interrogated me. They started to ask about my Visa, where I am coming from, and why I am visiting Macau solo? how much cash I have, etc. They also demanded to verify all things which I answered. They confirmed my documents, they counted my money, and everyone started looking at me like a criminal or potential problem maker.

Of Course, I was not prepared for it. As I said, we can never prepare perfectly for any journey, so all I did was be very calm and smile and answer everything politely as much as possible. Also, over-sharing some beneficial information like my host phone number/ my pictures in previous countries, my other visas in my Passport. Later, from interrogation, it converted into a friendly chat. We became so friendly that one of the customs officers even offered me his phone number for any issue I face in Macau.

These experiences, these memories will always go a long way in someone's life because when you go through these unknown situations which you could never be prepared for, you gain confidence, you build up a character to handle the unknown, whatever it may be.

Journey Builds Relationships

When you travel with someone or even solo, you face many situations where you have to act depending on your personality. Some situations are good, and some are not; however, your decision-making capacity is tested in both.

With all this, you know more about the people you are travelling with because every decision you take impacts the whole group of people you are travelling with.

When you travel with someone, you have ample time to make conversations on almost every topic in the world. People don't usually take particular time out to make the conversations they want because we have other important priorities in our day-to-day life. But these journeys are a great excuse to have those beautiful conversations and know the people you are with more and more.

This is the reason I genuinely believe that journey is far more important and amazing than the destination itself. A journey makes you learn a lot more than any destination. A journey builds up your character and relationships and creates an important impact in your life.

Travelling is undoubtedly one of the most beautiful and constructive experiences to have in life. For us who love to travel, every opportunity is good to leave our habits and leave for new places, cultures, and people.

The true and sincere reason why it is said that happiness is a journey and not the destination!

Songwriters and poets have always offered many phrases about happiness, giving different interpretations and infinite interpretations. But what is happiness really?

Some say it is a moment, and others think it is a point of arrival. Others still believe that happiness is seeing the good side of every situation. The truth is that each of us has our own idea of happiness because basically, no one can know better than you how you perceive things and what will make you happy as you like it.

Some would say that life is made up of many moments of suffering, representing the price to pay for a moment of happiness. But is it really worth it? If you try to shift the focus and see happiness as a journey, and not as a destination, as a moment, you quickly realize how much beauty there is in every day and that perhaps happiness lies in recognizing that beauty. Searching for beauty is a great reason to see happiness as a journey!

CHAPTER SEVEN

TRAVEL IS A REAL EDUCATION

Are travellers born or made?

There is no sure answer to this question. Still, it can be said that probably the truth lies somewhere in between: Wanderlust syndrome is rooted in our DNA, but at the same time, anyone can become a true traveller by putting world exploration on top of your priorities. There is a factor that helps to train a traveller from an early age, which is the support of parents. Having parents who love travel, adventure, and the outdoors allows you to grow up with irrepressible curiosity and the desire to discover lands near and far. Growing up with this approach is almost always synonymous with an adult life full of satisfaction and happiness.

It is a journey of pleasure and fun, an adventure journey, a journey into fantasy, a journey into space, and a journey to discover new cultures and new populations ...

The journey can be seen in many aspects, but for anyone who undertakes, it represents a life experience, good or bad, which brings about significant inner changes. After a trip, we feel endowed with a new richness that will also influence our daily life once we return home.

In fact, man has the beautiful ability to perceive and assimilate what is happening around him. It could be defined as an open drawer, capable of collecting within it many "bits" of a life lived, the fruits of his experiences, and thus he will find himself a "coloured," "multicoloured" man, a richer man.

His curiosity has always driven man to undertake adventure travel. There is talk of man's curiosity already in Homer's Odyssey in the figure of Ulysses, who wanted to discover what was beyond the Pillars of Hercules, the limit that was considered insurmountable.

Most people think that we are all capable of travelling. Who doesn't know how to take a plane and go to any place on the planet, stay for a while and come back? But this is far from the truth!

Travelling is an art. To distance yourself from the much simpler activity of going on vacation, you need some specific skills, good doses of awareness, and a little experience in the field. You can understand the difference between simple movement in earthly space and travel when you need what you put into practice while you are away from home, even when you return.

Creative activities are expressions of oneself; they emphasize the combination of various elements, the infinite possibilities. Travelling is one of these: the world offers its colours, and you compose them in your own way, a real work of art in which you end up finding yourself.

It can happen in a tiny hotel room on the edge of the known world or the busy streets of a large and famous metropolis. While on a rickety bus or the slopes of Sinai, It doesn't really matter where. If you travel, it happens sooner or later. And it is in that precise moment; you understand the scope and importance of the journey.

Perceiving the history of travel & mankind, we know that travel has mostly been a purposeful deed. People travelled to gather food, make the trade or with a completely different motive, to explore the land, to capture it perhaps, applicable to emperors/ colonists, or for the commoners it could be for experiencing a different environment, & thus it was primarily associated with one's livelihood & rejuvenation. But little do we consider "Travel" as a form of education.

Travel is one of the greatest practical education ones can have. Travelling is a set of experiences that can make your perceptions grow, vital in real-life education.

No one would deny what an open environment beyond a 4- walled classroom can teach us!! A few of the skills it teaches us are:

Management Skills

Be it managing time or money, the books or traditional style won't help you instil in you what's expected to learn for navigating through our lives. This kind of experience is best to revitalize in a real-life situation, e.g., Making A budget plan for the trip or the itinerary itself where you mould it to get the most out of the available resources, be it time, energy or money.

This is not an easy thing to do for beginners, but trust me, if you do this with some effort, there is never going back. This is also one of the primary reasons I implore everyone to take at least a few solo trips because when you are on your own, you are bound to learn management skills on the go. And even if you don't, you get to know the consequences for the same, which is a good thing because knowing where we are bad at is also a good thing.

Also, it's never about just planning things ahead of time and following them. On every step, you might have to improvise and handle it as per situation and country/ culture, language, currency.

This teaches you a lot about management. Isn't it amazing that you automatically become better and better at handling more life situations if you travel the world? This is the easiest way to grow your management skills!

Bringing the best out of Minimal

When on a trip, your mind always ticks to point you towards the "saving" ideas because of the scarcity of time or other resources we would have then.

On the same lines, I love a Youtuber called NasDaily who makes 1-minute videos around the world where he has made a video on 'Mountain Test.' Basically, his idea of knowing how much stuff exactly you need to carry around travelling is filling up a backpack and going up to a mountain. This test aims to understand that threshold and stick to it where you are comfortable carrying the backpack, which is easy for you to take even on higher grounds.

This test also implicates that having minimum luggage can help you travel anywhere with more ease. This may shock you if you perceive that travel means taking 100 clothes for pictures and tourist spots. But trust me, if you know how to travel anywhere with minimum stuff, your journey becomes more enjoyable and gives you more satisfaction with freedom and flexibility.

Helps one connect with & understand others

The more time you spend with others in their vicinity, the more time you have to know their story, their struggles & have chances to be a part of them or what they are going through, hence forming deeper connections you would have superficially formed at a distance.

Trust me, when you travel the world, you hear stories which you cannot even imagine—good, bad, ugly. As I have mentioned in my previous chapters, people are conversations, and conversations quickly turn about our lives, especially with people from different continents, countries, or places. The stories are raw, and they take you around the world without actually visiting that place yourself.

I have met people from Israel, Uzbekistan, and some countries most of us have not even heard of or know much about it. But when I listen to the stories and lives they have in some of these countries; I totally try to understand how it would feel if I had been in the same place.

This also makes you connected to other people.

Increases Confidence & Self-reliance & Discover Self

For travelling, one may need to pack on their own, plan on their own, or even during the travel; one needs to do a few or more things without relying on others beyond one's comfortable abode. This enhances an individual's ability to depend on no one but self & manage circumstances better at crucial times.

As I said before, when you travel, especially solo, you have to do everything on your own, and if you do it, it is a big booster for your confidence.

Think that you somehow travel Europe or South East Asia alone in countries where people do not speak English at all, and you rely just on your cell phone and common sense. It looks scary, right? But just for a moment, think, what if you can achieve this somehow! If you do it, then when you come back, you will have a different set of self-confidence to survive anywhere in almost any condition, given that you have some access to technology.

Also, when you travel the world, you discover yourself on the go. Sounds very cliche, right? But self-Discovery itself is a cliche.

Real-Life Simulation & Grasping concepts deeply

It teaches you in a very visual way, better to ingrain it deep & to last a long time. The best example would be Sonam Wangchuk's unique way of teaching through building or creating. If you know him, you might already know how he explained the concept of Water.

Conservation through Ice Stupas by building them and all through community activities; what if he'd have just written it in textbooks? Thus, being at a different place helps realize the unique characteristics geographically & in a very involved way. Similarly, learning is the best when supplemented with demonstrations or involvement in real-life experiences.

It is incredible to see movies, documentaries, or YouTube videos about any country or place in the comfort of your home, but being in the actual location can never be replaced with anything. It is not only about visuals or seeing those same things you have already seen on Video, but actually experiencing those places makes all the real difference inside your head and heart when you experience it with your real eyes!

Multi-dimensional Personality Development

Travel teaches us the necessary life skills to be successful individuals by allowing us to experience a situation with many possible takeaways. Few of which are highlighted below:

- Communication Skills

When you travel around, you have to speak to certain people irrespective of whether you are an introvert or an extrovert person. This makes you communicate your best, especially if you are travelling far away from your home where your language makes all the difference. The situations somehow teach you to communicate in your best interests and get things done.

- People Skills/ Social Engagement

When you travel in a group or travel solo, you are bound to interact with people everywhere you go. Adjusting with them automatically makes you better and better with Social Engagement. Even in the worst cases, you will always find others coming forward and talking with you if you must have to be an introvert.

- *Learn different languages & culture*

Do you know Shaking hands can be disrespectful in some countries? There are unimaginable cultures and languages out there, and everyone has their own way of everything from greeting to taking care of a guest.

According to Government guidelines, in some parts of the UAE, Kissing and holding hands is classed as "inappropriate behaviour." In some parts of Europe and Australia, you greet people with a kiss. Imagine how different countries make different cultures and, in turn, different behaviours.

This is amazing when you travel and meet people from other countries who tell you so many different and weird facts about different mindsets/ different beliefs/ different cultures. With all this, you realize that whatever you feel is right or wrong is a matter of relative perception and not the only truth.

Brings out creativity

When you see enough of the world and are a reasonable observer, you have no better education. When you visit different places worldwide implementing various solutions to the local problems, you learn a lot from understanding how creatively problems can be solved.

This is why a person who has travelled a lot will always tell you that if you implement this from that country, it would be great because a travelled person has many creative solutions being implemented in different parts of the world.

All of this boils down to giving an individual the opportunity to interact with people, communicate ideas, broaden perspectives, refresh, and experience everything first-handed; thus, **"TRAVEL FOR LEARNING BY DOING."**

Etiquette and Manners

I know it sounds funny, and you must think I am crazy if I say that we learn Etiquette and Manners from travelling. Maybe you are right about the crazy part, but trust me, we learn a lot about manners when we travel, especially abroad, because people at the airport/ lounge/ flights are on their best behaviour.

When people around you are at their best behaviour, you automatically mimic a bit and do not want to stand out by being an idiot. Think of a situation when everyone is giving away to an old lady to go ahead in a queue; you would probably not object if you are abroad because you will automatically feel obligated that you are representing the place where you are coming from, or you will not want to get unwanted attention and make a fool for yourself.

But given the same situation that happens with you here, locally, you would probably object or even fight if you are getting late.

So when we travel to different places, we are afraid about the culture and local practices; we feel obligated to represent the place we are coming from or do not want to get unwanted attention. This makes us behave at our very best and learn from our surroundings that everyone can follow and follow the trend.

Empathy

When you travel the world and check the places you have never been to, you see people living on very different standards than your home. When I was travelling to Cambodia and Laos, I met several people having an income of just a few dollars a day which was very hard for them. Coming from India, It was not much different seeing similar poverty, but sometimes when you know someone's problems far from you, you realize how you can help back in your home country.

Travelling makes you very empathic to others, and it changes you from the core of your heart. I am not saying only travel can make you empathic and nothing else, but when you travel, you are forced to see other people on streets, hotels, airports, bus stops which makes you wonder about them even if you have never been interested before.

There is no other education like Travelling

These are just some of the things travel can teach you, but apart from these, there are many things which you eventually start to learn when you travel. People spend so much on academic education; still, college can never teach anyone about real life. They can certainly increase your knowledge and memory power, but they can never teach you about exploring yourself first about different situations you can face. Of Course, Academic education is essential, but travel can teach you things that help you lead a better and peaceful life.

Why can the art of travelling change your life?

You learn to understand the diversity as a value and not as a problem. The mind becomes elastic and does not stiffen in the face of what it does not know. You develop the ability to be humble. Every traveller knows that his point of view is only one of many and no universal one. You exceed your limits, your east, your west, the mental architectural barriers that prevented you from thinking, 'I can' do it, I can't do it'. You learn to communicate in languages that are not yours. One day you wake up, and you realize you have your vocabulary, which talks about your travels, routes, and encounters.

Your awareness expands; you know you are something more than the work you do, the role you play. The world teaches you to laugh. Above all, about yourself, your beliefs, the ones you have always been attached to until the day you started travelling.

You do not judge a country after three days of stay and not even its inhabitants.

Instinct is reactivated; the senses are the doors through which you let what you meet in or out. You develop a strong sense of direction. You can also get lost and loiter, but you never feel lost. You capture every single moment; you value time as a space to live, as the only true wealth. You appreciate the little things those living in the west take for granted.

You discover your adventurous side you didn't even know you had, and you meet it while you feel free, without judgement about yourself. Some small phobias disappear. Maybe you were afraid of insects, and sleeping in a tent, you made it through. Or you keep the fear of flying with an anxiolytic in the bag at bay, but then you realize that the more you fly, the more the fear goes away. You value your life and its comfort every time you come back.

If you travel with someone and get along well with them, you develop the ability to meditate. Which perhaps is another art in itself.

No expectations about places, people, emotions. You let yourself be surprised and accept what you find.

You learn to eat everything. Despite being Indian.

When you visit different countries, you realise the food is never the same even if it looks the same or sounds the same. When you travel, you cannot expect to have the same taste or even flavours you eat back home and that really detaches you from having the similarity of what you usually eat. I have personally seen a lot of Indian people, including my friends struggling to be satisfied with the food they get outside their home country, but my friends, that is what travelling teaches you. Travelling forces you to adopt new cuisines which might be close to what you prefer to eat, but never the exact same and with that, you learn to not be dependent on the food you have always eaten. You learn to eat new things or at least you get a hard push to try them.

Then why would you miss such a fun & beneficial opportunity to learn?? Go Travel!

Action Items before you move to the next chapter:

• When you come back from the trip, make a rough list of what things you learned for the first time

• Write down the points which you think could have been dealt in a better way

• Write down the lessons you would share with your loved ones when they start travelling

CHAPTER EIGHT

BE A TRAVELLER, NOT A TOURIST!

The ray of life has once again emerged as people are starting to set themselves out free by going on trips after the deadly pandemic, we all faced. Thanks to the fewer restrictions imposed now on travelling, people can now relax amidst the COVID chaos & kind of break free from the trap due to lock-downs. Well, my family and I went on such a trip too. Sitting in the backseat of the car, enjoying the breeze, many thoughts came to mind, one of which was what makes a journey unique & memorable? The vague answer was people accompanying, experiences gained & new things tried, all of which shrunk down to qualities of a traveller & only traveller & not a tourist.

Well, you might be wondering what the difference between being a traveller & a tourist is? The base idea is one with an open mind, leaving comfort at home, carrying minimal items & always sitting on an edge, i.e., being eager to learn new things about people & places is a traveller!

One who becomes one with the place he goes to is a Traveller! While one who's being superficially at the place, like just visiting it, is a tourist.

While travelling, I was able to talk about the most diverse topics with hundreds of people of all ages, sexes, and nationalities. One topic that has come up many times, especially among travel enthusiasts, is the difference between being a tourist and a traveller.

The big discussion: Tourist or Traveller?

But is there a difference between being a tourist and a traveller? I think so, but at the same time, I am convinced that most people have not really caught it. Because listening to specific conversations or reading a lot of discussions on social networks, it seems that two factors determine this difference:

The cost of the trip & The destination.

Many are convinced that the tourist is simply the one who can spend a lot of money, while the real traveller is the one who travels at a low cost. The tourist is the one who visits certain places defined as "tourist" while the traveller is the one who sets out to go far and explore inaccessible areas, often poor, with few Western visitors.

So what is the difference between being a tourist and being a traveller?

As mentioned, I believe that there is this difference, but it does not concern the trip's cost or the destination. The real big difference is in the way a person behaves when travelling.

In my opinion, being respectful and humble means being travellers, while being ignorant, selfish, and extremely consumerist means being a tourist.

Perhaps it is not a distinction of immediate understanding, so I try to explain it better.

Who is the traveller?

The traveller is the one who is completely immersed in the reality that the tourist does not want to see. The traveller has the sole objective of discovering and is willing to do so by bringing the utmost respect for the places, traditions, and people he meets.

As I write in my chapter "Be a traveller, not a Tourist," the true traveller visits a place with the eyes of a child, the soul of a traveller, and the manner of a gentleman on a first date. It's all a question of respect, and who is respectful is a traveller. The traveller is he or she who eats local food, talks to the local people, slowly enters local customs and traditions. He does not consume but slowly savours every aspect of the new he is exploring. The traveller goes in-depth but leaves no traces of his passage: he tries to produce little waste, tries to keep the impact of his passage low and above all, actively contributes to preserving a place.

Here are some ways you can be a traveller & experience your trip a level deep:

Choose local cottages/Home Stays over 5-star hotels

This helps to be closer to learning about real life and people at a place. This also supports the locals there & gets you to understand & connect with them in a better way as given the more opportunities you get to interact with them. Thanks to technology, we have several websites now like Airbnb, Couchsurfing where you can find actual homes and not hotels. This allows you to stay at real, local houses, which were never possible before.

Not just booking, now you can get reviews from other people who have stayed there. You can know a lot more about the host, the area, and any type of feedback you are looking for. Imagine doing this in the 90s, it would have sounded crazy to write feedback for someone's real, local home, but today, you can book that within clicks and get into the local area of any country to explore its authentic culture and vibe.

As personal advice, I would recommend researching local homes from Airbnb more that have good reviews and are not very remote. As much as you want to experience local living, you also want to get out and check out the places you have already planned to.

Prefer community engagement over spas

No doubt if it's a leisure vacation, you would prefer to visit a spa, but if you're visiting a place to know about it genuinely, visit the local market places, town halls or attend any community events/gatherings if you come to know about it so that you know the cultural aspects & broaden your views.

Again, technology has made this job much more accessible than ever before. You can install Meetup Mobile App and find free and paid events in anything you like in any city in the world. If you are travelling in a strange country and want to meet decent people, say just for dinner or a movie or playing board games, Meetup has everything for you.

Apart from mobile apps, if you are staying in a hostel, ask them for local events in the area; they will guide you to the best local events, which might give you a true insight into a country or a city.

Prefer local guide over tourist guide/ packages

This is very important if you genuinely want to travel as a traveller and not as a tourist. I have seen many people visiting only tourist places and shying away from uncharted roads or areas. This is where the thin line comes between a traveller and a tourist. A tourist wants to stay in a 5-star hotel and look at only a few tourist places known to everyone.

On the other hand, a traveller enjoys more local taste by visiting places which are not so famous and unique. Of Course, to find these places, you just don't need time, but also an attitude of researching it with more odd options.

When I was visiting Lithuania in Europe, I kept digging places till I found something exciting. This place is called Hills of Crosses, a very off-road place in Lithuania's remote outskirts. To visit there, google maps showed me to change two buses and walk approx. 1-2 miles in the middle of nowhere. I did not find any public transport that would help me smoothly get there as a tourist.

But being a traveller, it was not a problem; it was a puzzle or a challenge I wanted to balance. So I started finding local tour companies and started calling them to ask if they could arrange a tour if I wanted to skip public transport and come back on the same day and from one number to another reference, I finally found a very small tour company which takes you to other location, but they also cover Hills of Crosses. I booked that tour around midnight for the very next morning and, to be honest, it was just a few euros more than what it would have cost me in Public Transport apart from time.

When I reached that place, It was just three other people and me on the whole damn Hill, and the feeling I achieved was something only a traveller can understand.

So I would really suggest finding some places which are amazing yet not much commercial. To do that, use extensive research and keywords to find different places in the country. Also, make local friends before you travel and ask them about those unique and non-commercial places.

Leave time for Impromptu plans

Make a flexible itinerary with considerable empty slots, which leaves you time to explore the locality & maybe go to the unplanned places. If you've no restrictions, you could make the whole trip unplanned as well, heading towards the direction your path & encounters lead to. I know this is ain't that feasible. But having such a trip once in a while, maybe every year completes your adventure/ thrill quota!

Even better, plan a trip with some special days for Impromptu plans. The reason for suggesting this is that travel basically means exploration. Unfortunately, due to time constraints, travel is becoming more like a redundant task for people. Everyone is supposed to plan each and everything in advance and then walk on that exact path like a robot irrespective of mood and vibe that specific day.

But planning some flexible blank days will make a good mix for your travel because you have some freedom to chase what you like after being in a city or country. Personally, I call them Blank Days, which I keep every 3rd day of my long-term travelling or even short-term.

I plan it rough for two days because I have to (Many countries do not give Visa to Indians unless they show a complete itinerary along with complete hotel and transport bookings); however, for the third day, I do not plan anything before travelling. Once I visit and explore in those first two days, I get an excellent idea about what could be an off-beat place I can explore, which I couldn't think of before, and then I try to either do that activity or relax on my bed sipping cocktails all day.

Immerse yourself in the local culture rather than standing out

This boils down to the saying: "Being a part of it & not apart from it," in numerous ways like adapting the local dressing style, language & accent, just the whole culture. Mind me doing this would add an altogether different version of you within your personality.

When I was in Bali, my friend cum tour guide Henni really pushed me to do this. She asked me to wear the local dress and take pictures and also be on the streets in that dress. In fact, she had a pair in her car ready which she gave me to wear. The experience of that is still unforgettable for me because when you indulge in local culture by dressing the local dress, visiting local cafes, and walking the local life, you really experience a different mindset and culture altogether. You feel you are not you, and there is someone new inside you who is doing all this.

Before travelling anywhere, I would suggest finding out the local dressing sense, the local dishes, the local market, and some cultural knowledge about the place. This helps you to be ready for a totally new experience if you are up for it.

I will show you what distinguishes a tourist from a traveller. And who are you on vacation?

The tourist already has an organized program. He has worked a whole year, has only one week of vacation, and wants everything to be perfect. For this, he often relies on others. Only rest, zero thoughts.

The traveller organizes his program. Sometimes it doesn't even have it. He wants a journey that belongs to him and made in his image and likeness. He does not follow patterns, only instinct.

Undergo a journey, not a vacation

As emphasized earlier, be on foot to welcome all the troubles/ un-comforts & enjoy the process of tackling them rather than just being a lazy panda or concerning much about your trip photos. Although photographs are a great way to take away the memories of the trip, yet for every minute you spend on adjusting while posing for a 48 MP camera, you're wasting the 60 seconds by not capturing the place's beauty by a 576 MP view your eyes would have captured.

Also, as I have said, the journey is always more important than the destination. Travel is a journey not just towards any city or country, but towards yourself first. When you take any journey as a journey, you explore yourself more than any other thing outside of you. You get into those moments where you see yourself so clearly, so crystal like it's someone else.

So always choose places which you feel will be close to your heart rather than other factors.

Explore local cuisines

This is a kind of the must-follow, untold rule of being a traveller. I prefer local food over regular hotel food at least a few times on the trip. A true traveller never misses the unique delicacies of the place!

For many, including me, sometimes local food seems crazy and ugly. But trust me, if you do not try local food and come back, you will always regret it because local food is something very unique you cannot buy in your home country even with any money you spend, and even if you can, it is never the same as origin.

So before you travel anywhere, make sure to check out local dishes and places to eat. With so many websites around, you are bound to get the best places to eat and names of local dishes first hand, even with a bit of research.

Understand the uniqueness

Know their specialty, unique challenges, and ideas to overcome them to become part of the place and gain invaluable knowledge & skills. Feel closer & experience genuine bonds, make connections for life, extend your family. Enjoy being one with nature. Fortunately, the world is a beautiful place to explore, and every land is different in one or another way. Some areas are purely artificial, and some places are naturally beautiful. But in each of the places, there is something unique and marvellous to look for.

If you google unique places in the world, you will be shocked at what the world has to offer because from magical temples to ghost towns, from purely artificial ski to natural hot water springs, you will get everything in this beautiful world.

It's a good idea to research these places if you are travelling far from your home. You might be surprised to know that some of the unique places do not necessarily mean they are commercial. Some unique places are far, and only a few people have documented it, so it's an excellent chance to make one hell of an exciting story for your friends when you come back.

You Represent Your Country

Just as "Wherever we go becomes part of who we are", the place changes by our presence too, so make sure you leave a piece of you there, could be tiny as anything like leaving a smile over one's face, making someone feel a strangers' love, connection, humility, or even sharing about your culture/ ideas.

Remember, if you are travelling to another country as a traveller, you are not in a group of people, and so you alone represent the land where you are coming from. If you behave well and leave a good impact on people by just being polite, calm, and reasonable, people are not just going to think good about you, but also the country you are coming from.

When you stay in hostels or meet people anywhere, the first few greetings are always about your location, your culture. Though everyone is a very different human being, and no one can be judged on the land they are coming from, there are certain everyday things between people of the same land. A simple example is that if you are coming from a developed country, drinking tap water directly would be normal for you, but you will take time to comprehend this thought if you are coming from emerging countries.

Similarly, when we do things somewhere else, it represents our trends and culture and not just us individually.

Real Difference

Learn this simple analogy: "Anyone who needs more than 1 suitcase is a tourist & not a traveller!"

The tourist seeks comfort. At the cost of carrying the entire wardrobe, tourists want to feel at home. He does not want unexpected events, setbacks, or nasty surprises. It is your well-being at the centre of the holidays.

The traveller seeks adventure. Here is one of the main differences: the traveller wants to experience the place; it is the place that is visiting the absolute protagonist of the trip. Look for the surprise, the unexpected: it will be the next anecdote to tell friends and relatives once back.

The tourist sees a place. He has a fixed program that he plays together with many other people. His entire itinerary is studied down to the last detail to show him the best and in the best possible way—everything at your fingertips, often from behind a window.

The traveller experiences a place. He gets lost in the city streets and, even if he doesn't visit a museum, he will be right: maybe the coffee at the bar with the older man from the village was a more interesting experience. He touches everything with his hand and feels it.

Tourists can't wait to show photos of themselves on vacation. Back home, the tourist will show friends and relatives his photos posed in front of the hotel, near that famous monument, the selfie in the main square. He is the protagonist and makes no secret of it.

The traveller will show you photos of what he saw. Seeing them won't seem particularly beautiful or interesting, but for the traveller, they were essential. Maybe he photographed a child intent on playing, a woman hanging out the laundry on the balcony, or a cat at the door. Here are the differences: the traveller is only interested in the experience he is having.

The tourist will always choose the safest route. You will hardly see a tourist on public transport or improvise something. No matter the price: safety and convenience are priorities, and he is unwilling to give them up.

The traveller will always prefer discovery. He is always looking for unexplored paths and trails. Its priorities are adventure and, above all, low cost. He knows that, by doing so, he will be able to discover breath taking landscapes and unrepeatable panoramas.

These are the main differences, and who knows how many others you can find. Obviously, we know that they are a bit of cliché and also a bit of prejudice. All of us in life have sometimes been tourists, sometimes travellers. No matter who you are, the important thing is to travel (respecting the environment)!

For travelling is looking beyond what's right in front, living an unexplainable experience that has changed you by bits.

CHAPTER NINE

Make Friends Around the World

It sounds so cool to have friends around the world, right? It is cool to know that you have people you can call friends and catch up with them being from different parts of the world! The best part about this thing today is that anyone can do it with technology and some patience.

When you travel solo or even with groups, there are certain ways to meet people, and trust me; if you are looking to make friends, it's easiest to do so in hostels because the vibes are so friendly. Even hostels arrange many events, which are group activities or bonfires or just casual game rooms where people come and meet each other.

The big question, even after reading this, remains: How? How can you utilize the ways and means to meet better people and be safe at the same time? How can you know if people are good enough to be trusted and not some hippies who would sell you anything?

Well, there are always two ways in today's world, one with technology and one with traditional. Both are fun.

Mobile Apps

Trust me, it sounds absurd, but technology is a game-changer when it comes to meeting people around the world, even if you do not travel. Today, so many applications help you connect people in whatever part of the world you are interested in. Yes, there are many cases where you meet the wrong kind of people or people who pretend to be someone else and are not really that but isn't that how the actual world works? Applications are not the problem. Bad people are the problem. If a person is into cheating, he will do it even in the physical world; yes, apps make it easier for him, that is why when using these apps, we have to be a bit more cautious. Some of my suggestions would be as below:

- *Meetup*

This is one of the safest applications I have used to meet safe and like-minded people. This application is a place to network on similar topics of your choice. For example, you are interested in meeting only people who share a common interest in Chess. So you go on a website, choose your city or location you are currently in, and find out about upcoming meetups related to Chess. Obviously, there are chances that you will sometimes not find the meetups coming up as per your interest or dates. Still, at least you have a better probability of finding it here rather than searching it anywhere else.

Also, the best part about this app is that anyone can host meetups for free. So if you are interested in exploring the nearby lake on the weekend and want to go with someone with a similar interest, you can create an event for free. When someone searches about it in the same location, they will be shown this event, and they can contact you to take it further. All for free!

- *Tinder*

Many dating apps are famous, and every day, there are hundreds of more applications, but I think Tinder is more than just a dating app. Because of its features and popularity, you will find many, many people on Tinder just looking for casual meetups and nothing more. If you are interested in meeting someone interesting who is also local or expat, you can always look up people and, if you get a match, can ask for coffee, being a decent person. More than half the time, if you are decent enough, you will get someone for coffee or a walk in the park, and you have a great chance to build up a connection. You just have to be a bit more aware on Tinder as you can't know much about a person till they themselves help you do that. Always video call the person before you agree to meet up.

- *Couchsurfing*

This is a great website to stay for FREE and make friends around the world. So this is basically a website for travellers who understand other travellers' needs and help them get a place for free. Here is how it works:

You live in a city or the great countryside, and you have a spare couch or a room in spare. You will go on this website and list your details about letting anyone stay at your spare place for free. In this, you are anyway not paying extra for that person, but in return, you get two things: A great friend around the country or world and also great official feedback on the website.

Now imagine the tables are turned, and you decide to travel anywhere in the world. You go to this same website, find a place, and ask them to let you stay for a couple of days. The first thing they would look at is your reviews because they would want to know what type of a person you are, and if you had hosted any people with good experiences, the chances are you will get anyone to host you. This circle goes on, and this way, you meet friends around the world, either being a host or asking other hosts to host you in different places.

- *Local Hostel Apps*

Nowadays, there are more hostel chains meaning they are not only present in one country, but some hostel chains are present all around the world in all major countries. This gives you similar benefits you get from any brand. You understand how it works even if you have never been to all the countries they operate in because brands like to work similarly anywhere they go to make all customers more comfortable.

These hostels now have gone much ahead and made everything online, from check in's, verifications, extending your stays, changing your beds to asking for help, and check-out routines as well. Apart from all functional things, they have also added options to find people from the same hostel to hang out or go to parties together. This becomes a huge attraction for solo travellers as they can now use the same hostel app and find friends of similar interests without going anywhere out. So it's always a great idea to ask these things from reception if you are travelling solo, so you can download these local hostel apps and maybe find someone probably on the same floor.

- Dating Apps for Singles

Well, there was a time when we all had to go clubbing to find new friends or people of similar interests, but today, technology has changed everything. Now, just from your home, you can try to make friends from anywhere in the world without even travelling to those places in person. Again, this is debatable if it's a good thing or a bad thing, but if you use it with caution, it's a great idea.

These days, there are so many amazing apps out there that have different mechanisms to meet other people. Some apps filter and find you people based on location proximity, and some apps find you people with similar interests, and then there are so many apps that use mix and match models.

If you are travelling solo, dating apps could be entertaining to meet locals and hang out with them only if you take proper caution and do not meet people in isolated places or trust anyone easily. But if you know to get these precautions, you might find a charming person to take local trips with.

Physical places

Given that the world is already living most of the time in the digital world, our minds are not made to accept that easily because the fundamental core nature of a human being is based on touch, feel, and connection with other human beings. So even if hundreds of apps may make people meet, they are just the tools to get to the point of the meeting. So if you are not a person who likes to filter things and downsize your arena, there is always the best way to meet others: The traditional way!

It's exactly the thing which we would have all done sometimes in our life, meeting someone at a party, meeting someone in a museum, or a club or a game room. The best thing about meeting people traditionally is that there is always an element of surprise. You never know how the person is, what they like, or what they would think about certain things. There will always be a magic element that will keep you curious and on edge if there is a connection.

Beyond all the adventures and memories, what makes travelling, so fun is meeting new people and making friends from all over the world. Travellers, hikers, and globetrotters all know what it's like to be in a place where you don't know anyone, so they are generally very friendly, and starting a conversation is usually very easy. However, there are two types of people globally: those who need to open their mouths to make friends and others who need a little help to get out of their comfort zone. To simplify the whole friendship process a little, it is essential to have an open and curious mind and to do something fun and of your interest. Preferably, in one of these below mentioned places:

These are the few places I have met people traditional way and have been strong friends ever since:

- Hostels

Hostels are by far the best places to meet others without making much effort. If you choose to live in dorms, it's a culture to greet each other and know more about each other. This becomes so normal that you automatically feel that you already have friends wherever you go. Hostels also have a reception that is familiar with requirements and culture that can help you or guide you to direct to events hosted by them for this same purpose because one of the best pleasures of travelling is knowing how amazing people are from around the globe!

Many hikers and people travelling alone decide to stay in hostels, which tend to be cheaper than hotels. For this reason, you will find yourself amid many people with an open mind and in welcoming situations, such as breakfast in a large hall or group activities that will make it easier to fit in with other people. Plus, they usually all have great travel tips, which is why it's definitely worth a conversation with them no matter where you are.

- Live with the locals

Of course, you can't just knock on someone's door and ask them to let you in, invite you to lunch, and become your friend. But there are hundreds of opportunities to immerse yourself in a new culture, living by local customs, from Couchsurfing to Airbnb. Living in an apartment or house is, in fact, a great way to start discovering a city, and meeting people, neighbours, and locals.

- *Volunteer*

Why not do something good for your soul and the local community through volunteering? This experience will not only help you improve the world by giving something back to the place you will be staying with, but it will also allow you to immerse yourself in its culture and interact with people who are involved in an important cause (and let's not forget that it is a beautiful way to follow or discover your passion).

- *Cafes/ Bars*

This, of course, is much more common than the above options! Cafes and bars are some nice places to meet people if they are structured in that way. I remember that I was in South Asia, and there was this cafe for people who want to meet others where you basically order for yourself, but you will get some different dishes. Later you will know who ordered that and you have to exchange the dish with that person. This gives you a fantastic way to talk with new people about cuisine!

- *Bus/Train Stations/Airports*

These places are really great places to have conversations and maybe make friends going to the same place as you are! I remember making so many friends at the airport and bus stations who were also headed to the same place. It is usually easy to spot solo travellers or group travellers at Airports, making it very easy to approach and start talking.

Even on Airplanes, I have met several people who started talking about travel plans, and it turns out that there is so much new information exchanged.

- Go on an excursion or some recreational activity

Many hotels, schools, and cities offer tours, excursions, and various activities for free or at affordable prices. This will help you explore your new home and give you an accurate understanding of where you will be and which you won't find in any book. Usually, these are sightseeing tours and group activities, so you will be surrounded by other people you can talk to and take some selfies with. Who knows, maybe you'll end up trying that restaurant you passed by before or continue exploring together.

- Contact your circle of friends

If you have friends (or friends of friends) who have recently been to, for example, Europe/India, contact them to see if they may have any suggestions. Who knows, they might recommend a number of things to do or even put you in touch with some of their local friends who you can meet for a coffee or a sightseeing tour.

- Become a regular customer

If you stay in a given city for a while and keep going to the same restaurant or cafe, the staff will start to recognize you sooner or later. This will be a great chance to have a chat or get helpful advice on things to do, and mostly the waiters are used to making conversation, introducing people, or helping customers, so there's a good chance you can even do or see some of those things together.

- *Eat and drink*

We all need to eat and drink, and choosing the same restaurant or bar is already something we have in common. Just look for someone else who is eating alone. Of course, it could be risky because maybe the person in question really wants to eat alone, but nothing prevents them from approaching and saying: "Hello! I see you are eating alone, and I was wondering if I could join you" There is nothing to fear: get out of your comfort zone, and you could have an enjoyable conversation.

What's in it for you?

You might wonder about the benefit of making friends while travelling as they will not meet you again anyway, isn't it? Well, you never know for sure! I met some friends in Paris who were originally from Taiwan, and we connected well.

When I planned to travel to Taiwan, I realized how important that friendship turned out for me. He helped me explore local Taiwan and gave me unique information that only locals can do. Apart from local travel, the most significant benefit I had was a sense of security by having someone local as your friend whom you can trust to help in case you get stuck anywhere.

So it is really beneficial to have friends around the world if you are a true traveller or even if you are just interested to know different cultures and stories of people around the globe.

Benefits

There are so many benefits to having cool friends around the world.

- You can always know what's happening on the other side of the world, which sometimes news does not cover

- You can rely on a local person and take help for planning your trip if you are making any travel plan for that country

- You might get a place to stay in case they have a spare room when you travel to their country

- You can always take help for something that is not otherwise easy doing remotely, like getting some product from that country or maybe knowing something.

- You will be amazed to know so many different cultural things if you follow them on social media, and the best part is that you can always connect to them and ask more about it in detail.

CHAPTER TEN

21st Century Let's You Earn Anywhere

Yes, believe it or not, we never had this many opportunities in the world we have today. The Internet and technology have changed almost every aspect of our lives and how we live! We no longer have to write letters and wait for weeks to get answers, we no longer have to walk thousands of miles to meet someone, we no longer have to have extra space at home to keep physical books. Technology has changed everything from how we work to how we enjoy our leisure time.

With so many changes in the world, now anyone can actually do things that might have seemed a superpower some decades ago. Today a person can be in Europe and handle a business having clients in America by making his employees work in India! Do you realize how amazing that is? It isn't any less than magic or a superpower!

With this, the world has become a closer, connected, and powerful place. Today, anyone with access to computers or mobile can learn a skill in a couple of months which can help him earn by providing those services on freelance websites or corporations. There was never a time like this where our college degrees were optional. There was never a time in history when people thought they could get jobs or earn good enough without having more degrees or ample struggle. But all this has been changed in the 21st Century.

21st Century is not less than a beautiful fairy tale where you read about people making millions of dollars from a ten-by-ten room. This is a century where you will hear about people making a full-time income by just giving out extra rooms in their homes on Airbnb. There are so many people who are making a decent income by only using one skill of driving and getting themselves registered on Uber. There are people getting rich by investing in virtual currency, NFT's, etc which was an alien concept few years ago.

Time has changed so incredibly that today if someone tells you something crazy, you would not feel it's crazy enough. This has also led every one of us to have more freedom in our lives. In the history of human civilization, there was no time like this where people could sit at home or travel full time and still have enough to live a decent life.

Coming back to the impact on travel, it is huge. It is more than you think. The travelling industry has changed tremendously in the 21st Century. Travel which was considered a luxury thing for rich people is now something anyone can experience. Not only just experience, with some efforts, maybe make a full-time profession. There have been thousands of different ways to earn by travelling, via travelling, along with travelling, or just being indirectly related to travelling.

Below are some ways you can earn even if you travel for extended time periods. Unlike old times, you do not have to depend only on the regular job or business for your growth and survival.

Working in Hostels

This is one of the best odd jobs you will do if you don't mind exchanging your skills for free food and bed while travelling long term. This not only saves a lot of money but also gives you a great experience to mingle with people around the world, all while getting a free bed and free food. Many online portals will help you do this legally and with trusted hosts/guests. One of my favourites is https://www.workaway.info/

This website has been there for a very long time and has a great reputation in this community. Of course, with the growing community, many other websites offer these types of services and allow users to have more functions. This is how it works:

1. You register on the portal with the skills you possess. Skills can be anything simple from speaking English or two languages to Complex with the specific skill of carpentry or IT.

2. You get verified through the system they have

3. You select the country, the city where you want to travel and work

4. Checkout listed hostels in the area you desired and read all the requirements carefully

5. Contact the Host/Hostel with your profile for any questions you have

6. Request to work there for a period of your time you desire

7. Once Accepted, take care of your visa and flights and reach the hostel to start your travel+work

It is one of the beautiful experiences anyone can achieve without going through traditional job finding services in a strange new country abroad.

Working Remotely

It took Pandemic to help us realize how amazingly most of the jobs related to technology can be done from anywhere in the world without even stepping out foot outside of your home. Of course, nothing is perfect, and working remotely has its pros and cons, from taxation to productivity point of view. But hey, we are talking about making things happen to live on our terms; that would require a new perception anyway.

There are many job roles which we will discuss in just a min which are completely remote and can be done from anywhere in the world as long as you have good internet and a functional laptop. There are great websites on which you can sign up to get started even when you are learning those skills and can help. Some of the great websites on which I have personally worked are:

https://www.fiverr.com - This one is one of my favourites due to the worldwide traffic it has, and almost everything is possible on this website. You can sell your skills from $5 to $500+ and create your portfolio. The flow from getting an order to completion of the order is excellent on this website, and there is always a support team to help if something goes wrong. The automatic notifications/templates, etc., are great for beginners to start selling any good skill.

https://www.freelancer.com - This one has the most extensive network of freelancers in the world, with millions of jobs posted every month. They have many different models for applying for jobs in whatever skill sets you are looking at. This is a great place to understand the market and what sort of jobs you would be getting once you are good at specific skills.

https://www.upwork.com - This one is basically a bit of a mixture of the above websites but with great filters and hard verifications of clients and freelancers. This website also helps you work on an hourly, weekly, or task basis with easy configuration, and payment systems are very smooth for almost every country in this world.

https://www.flexjobs.com - This portal helps you find remote full-time jobs from all over the world. The best part of this website is that they do the hard work to search, refine and post all jobs posted in different places over a single platform.

Working in Bars

It's obviously odd at first to imagine working in a bar in a foreign country while travelling but trust me if you have some experience in Bar jobs, this is the best temporary job one can do for a short time while travelling. This job not only gets you inside some of the best clubs but also quickly helps you make friends smoothly. These days, most tourist places look for people who can work for free in bars in exchange for meals/stay or small pay, but that is a win-win for both parties, travellers, and a bar owner.

Although this is a job where you need excellent skills to manage money, make drinks, an intensive knowledge of alcohol and different drink types, if you are fortunate to learn it, it will be worth it in the long run of world travelling.

The Future is Remote!

Although the transition to working from home was fast and furious for many organizations, many companies are now figuring out that **working remotely is the future of work—pandemic or not.**

"I want to have a good job, but I also want to have a life." This sentence sums up one of the most important statements of Millennial and Gen-Z workers. These are the fastest-growing, most prevalent groups in the workforce today, which means it's not a sentiment to take lightly. In fact, it can be argued that younger workers are dramatically changing the way we work, based on the current and projections on the future of remote working.

Today, more than ever before, people are working in places outside of the conventional office. Coworking spaces are a booming industry all their own, established corporate giants are adopting hot desk policies, and some companies exist entirely thanks to a telecommuting workforce. Going to a job, sitting at a desk for eight hours, and going home at the end of the day is no longer the undisputed norm.

Remote working isn't a novel concept. It's been around for as long as people have travelled for work. The recent rise of remote working is largely technology-driven since collaboration via cloud systems is so prevalent. The future of remote work will be dictated by a younger generation of workers intent on working to live instead of living to work.

Further, into the future, the focus will shift to a 24-hour work cycle. Just as we have a 24-hour news cycle, globalized markets and the shift to flexible work arrangements will create a full-day work cycle. Night owls will work the second and third shifts. Traditional workers will stay on first and second shifts. And, because everyone can work at preferred times, a company can reasonably expect some form of operation at all hours—without the cost of keeping a physical office open.

While no one knows exactly what the future has in store, it's all but certain remote working will play a significant role in how the workplace will evolve in the coming years. More than that, it's sure to continue changing the way we work.

This is great news for people like you and me who want to earn good money and keep exploring the world on our terms. Think of a day that is not a distant dream anymore where you are sipping fresh lime on a beach in your pyjama, all while attending a meeting. This will increase productivity and creativity to get more done in less time without taking leaves for travel.

Get Skills for Remote Work for Long Term Travel

Unfortunately, not all jobs can be done remotely. If you are in hospitality, factory work or coaching, athletes, then working remotely is not an option for you. Although partial things can be done, there could be a lack of inefficiency. So if you want to travel the world without leaving your job, you can start acquiring some of the skills which are easy to learn and practice in your spare time. Slowly these new skills can be put to use and grow into full-time work.

There are hundreds of different jobs which can be done remotely, but few of these are well established worldwide:

- *Developer/IT Consultant/Web Developer*

Developer/IT consultants are in high demand, and this is one of the best roles which can happen remotely. All you need is Laptop and Internet.

Not only are developer roles frequently remote, but there's also massive demand for these positions making these roles top remote jobs. Because of this, remote jobs in the development realm don't mean working for lesser-known companies or taking a pay cut. In fact, it might mean the opposite.

The tech industry will only grow, and there will only be more demand for developers and engineers. If you're not already a developer, there are many free resources available to help you build your skills for free. From there, you can jump into an internship or junior developer role and work your way up.

Millions of courses and resources today can help you learn different languages and tools and even help you get certified. Even this can be done completely remotely without any traditional teaching.

- *Digital Marketing*

Are you good at selling? If you answered yes, perhaps a Digital marketing role is the one for you. Online Marketing a catch-all term for many different skills that come under the marketing umbrella. Some of the different areas of expertise include working in search engine optimization (SEO), search engine marketing (SEM), affiliate marketing, content marketing, or email marketing, requiring a different set of skills. However, as it's related to technology and not traditional marketing, it all can be done remotely from anywhere in the world.

Remote marketing jobs are becoming easier to come by, especially as Digital marketing roles generally require very little specialist equipment. Because there are so many different marketing areas, there are plenty of opportunities for you to refine your skills in one area and look for remote jobs in that space. You can start for small companies providing your skills for free to gain more experience, which might land you good jobs.

- Writer/Editor/Translator

With the internet connecting us all, the demand for translators has only increased and not decreased even with the automatic online tools. Businesses are eager to bridge the communication gap between users of different languages. A translator can work a variety of different roles, such as working testing websites, translating documents, or proofreading.

Obviously, this is a remote job that requires you to have very high language skills in at least two languages. And if you are proficient in multiple languages, this would give you more scope. However, if you do happen to be at least bilingual, some translation remotes jobs may suit you. If you are starting or studying in university, you can utilize the extra time to learn a new language and practice, which can land you great remote opportunities as a full-time job or even freelancer.

- Customer Support

If you've got a way with people and love working to solve problems, a customer support role is one of the remote jobs that would suit you. Many jobs in this industry might interest you, from product selling companies to specific services selling industries. Working in this role requires you to use call or chat software to answer customer questions and solve problems.

To excel in this role, you need to have excellent communication skills and quickly learn about the product or service you will be helping customers with. While some customer support roles are full-time positions, others may be part-time or weekend or evening work. This makes it easy to work around other commitments you may have. This also gives you the benefit of having cross-cultural interactions. This might need better internet connectivity than other jobs, but you can always allocate fixed working hours in these types of jobs.

- *Teacher/Language Teaching*

Teaching Language is already a very common job for travellers, but you may not know that teaching also makes to the list of remote jobs. With the help of a stable internet connection and a headset, you can easily start online teaching and help students with their language skills. I have met many people in hostels wearing headphones and speaking Spanish or English, and when I ask them, they are usually teaching some kids far off the country from the comfort of the bunk bed in a hostel.

English and Spanish teachers are always in demand, but there's also a need for many different languages worldwide. To be a great teacher, you need to have excellent communication skills, be organized enough to put together lesson plans, and have a genuine interest in your students' development. However, nowadays, the teaching websites themselves help you plan lessons and use pre-defined researched templates for better teaching.

- *Virtual Assistant*

Ready to help entrepreneurs and businesses get organized? Becoming a virtual assistant is a role that does just that. This is one of those remote jobs that helps take off some pressures on others by taking on simple but time-consuming tasks.

A virtual assistant may perform customer service duties or fulfil orders for online stores. They might also make small updates and changes to websites or handle calendars. To be a virtual assistant, you need to be responsible, organized and have excellent communication skills. Virtual assistant roles aren't necessarily full-time, which leaves a lot of flexibility. If you have time constraints, being a virtual assistant is one of the best part-time remote jobs.

- *Social Media Manager*

If you're searching for remote marketing jobs that will allow you to utilize all your social media skills, you should look into social media manager roles.

A social media manager position can easily be done from home as you communicate with your team via chat or email and schedule your posts using online tools. Having an excellent grasp of the different social media platforms and what content does or doesn't work is a must. However, you can build these skills over time. Start by helping a small company and then use that experience to gain work with bigger businesses. So don't think your usage of Social Media is a complete waste. If you are smart, you can make a career out of this.

The best part of the 21st Century is that there are changes every day, and there are new streams every day, which would have been crazy even to think a few decades ago. If you are genuinely inspired to travel, this is the best time ever where you can travel and work together.

CHAPTER ELEVEN

Experience vs Things

Have you seen those people who do not have any savings to buy cars and apartments but have many stories to tell? I am certainly one of them, and this is an answer to everyone who has a question of whether we should possess things or experiences? What lasts longer? What is worth more? A trip around the world or a luxury car for the whole family?

Sounds Absurd? Right? I mean, the answer to the question is, of course, 'Things.' But if you think it through, you would remember your experiences more than what you had five years back.

First, I would say we probably would agree on one point: life is very short and we are given a limited amount of time to do anything we want, and we certainly cannot do everything we want to.

Being said that, we always tumble to question and always compare between taking that trip which will cost a Couple of Hundred Dollars or buying that 4K TV which costs the same, the only difference being is former will last five days and later will last for at least three years. But what if I tell you, a trip for five days is worth more than the latest

TV? Would you agree? I hope you do!!

Research shows we cherish experiences more than material things because experiences make us feel that possessing things cannot.

There is a common observation among family and friends that when they feel low, they always see pictures of trips, travel and wish they could live that moment again. Yet, no one looks at an iPhone and says, 'Well, I have the best phone, so this should make me feel good even though it's old' because the happiness of buying things lasts for a fraction of time compared to the happiness of having some non-materialistic experiences.

What is it about the nature of imagining experiential purchases that's different from thinking about future material purchases? The most interesting hypothesis is that you can imagine all sorts of possibilities for an experience. "There is an end number of ways your experience will go," but with material possession, you kind of know what you're going to get, which makes your material possession limited to a number of ways it could turn out.

The question might arise, so should we just spend all on experiences and not possess the things we want? The answer would not be simple because that depends on what kind of a person you are. I think the best answer would be to live life with a lot of experiences and little things rather than doing vice versa because, in the end, you are not going to take things with you, you are going to need some stories to smile on your deathbed.

Tie Happiness to Your Thoughts, Not Things or Experiences

We always are happy when we buy something or when we experience something, aren't we? But have you ever noticed that we are always living in a loop running for things and experiences in exchange for some happiness, some feelings of bliss! But what if we could break the loop?

Now, I am not saying for one moment that buying happiness with things and experiences is wrong or It can completely stop; however, my point is, will we ever achieve all the things and experiences on any day that we think about moving beyond that? It's worth giving a shot to think about this!

From what we have seen and learned about the world, the answer would be close to no, because if we don't become happy with things and experiences, what else is left in the world to be happy about? I would say thinking process, thoughts, mindset. Because with increasing choices and an increasing number of exposures to things and experiences we didn't even know existed, we all are living in a world of 'The Paradox of Choice,' which basically means an abundance of choice often leads to depression and feelings of loneliness along with a fear of either being left out of some experience or things which you think is necessary for your happiness.

I would love to explain this with a simple example that probably we all can relate to. Wherever you go by a cafe or restaurant in far off places where you are informed that only 3-5 things could be served, making your choice much limited, but have you noticed that your decision is much faster and satisfactory because you don't have the feeling of trying the best out of 100 things. Similarly, in other situations, when you go to a café where there are thousands of choices, it often leads to a longer time to decide, and even after your decision, if you look around someone having something much better, you think you would have made a different choice or maybe you could have thought more what was best for you. Now, this, we face in everyday situations.

With gigantic exposure to the world via Internet, social media, etc., we are always in 'The Paradox of Choice', where we think that we are not complete without these things or experiences, or we cannot be happy. A simple example would be people lining up for the latest gadgets like iPhones, iPods, etc. because companies have made sure to make you feel incomplete without their products or services, which you might have never wanted in the first place.

So, I think our happiness has moved from trying to be content with what we have to try to cover more and more experiences or buy more and more stuff, which I think is not the right approach to be happy or content.

Rather, what if we slowly and eventually try to change our thought process of thinking simply what is a need and what is not. So, to explain this, maybe why not attack our insecurities of being left out, or being incomplete, or being low in social status without certain unnecessary things, experiences which most of the time are just for a show and not personal contentment.

Being an avid traveller, I am not saying for one moment that we should give up everything and every experience and try to be happy without it, it's not possible either, but what I am trying to say is, why not change the priorities with mindset to have more contentment than more quantity of things and experiences. You might be a rich person who is not satisfied with the iPhone 9 because you want the latest one even though nothing affects your necessary needs. Still, you might also be another rich person who is content with iPhone 6 if it works for you and does not hurt your work/personal life in any way. So, what is the difference between these two people? The Mindset, the thought process!

I think if we change the process of being happy from more things/experiences to more prioritized needs, also prioritized things and experiences, we would be more content with less and falling less for 'The Paradox of Choice' because now the happiness will not be tied with the quantity of things/experiences you can have or do, but rather the quality of things and experiences you actually love which are equal sources of contentment. And the best part of all this is, you can do it with just a change in your mindset! (Maybe time-consuming, but worth giving a try)

So, sometimes we need a little push to travel. Being happier is probably the best reason to pack up and leave.

Here you will find some reasons or mindsets why we should travel the world more and why we can be happier doing that.

1. Get to know new cultures, because happiness is contagious

We understand the world better when we discover new cultures. All over the world, on every mountain, behind every river, among all the forests, a new and exciting culture awaits us. New cultures can enrich us and give us a whole new world view. Taste new food, experience new traditions, and dance new dances. These are all experiences we can have on the go. It doesn't matter if we walk in hiking shoes, sandals, or high heels. It is important always to be open to new things to broaden your perspective on the world.

2. Learn a new language - Share happiness with international friends

How do you learn or improve a language faster than practicing abroad? Sometimes we have to jump beyond our shadows to talk to strangers to get perfect language practice. It's a big step in the beginning. Still, it gets smaller over time as long as we will have smooth conversations in different languages in a completely natural way and without difficulty. The experience of exchanging exciting and unusual topics with people worldwide is wonderful and worth an adventure.

3. Gain self-confidence - Radiate happiness

Each journey is an adventure with which new challenges come to us. We are in a completely new environment, we find ourselves among many new people, and we don't wake up every morning in our comfort zone. Everyone probably knows that on vacation, you find yourself in a very different situation every day. In these moments, we continue to develop and discover new sides for ourselves. During a journey, of course, we also experience negative moments that challenge us. By facing these moments, we become braver, more confident, and we know ourselves.

4. Volunteer abroad: Help make yourself happy

Volunteering abroad is not a journey in the original sense, but it brings the same benefits, if not more. We learn to use a language better, and we learn to understand cultures better. We jump over our shadows and build self-confidence. So we can share the happiness we feel on the journey. At the same time, we help other people, animals, or nature. Volunteering helps not only others but also ourselves because it is an experience of a lifetime.

5. Make international friends - because friendship is just another word for happiness

The friends you travel with or the friendships you make while travelling are mostly friendships forever. All memories and all experiences lived together are special and weld together. Being around the world means being exposed to oneself and one's thoughts, which intensifies the emotions. Especially in a group or partnership, travelling together often leads to greater cohesion because we grow together with our tasks. And what's more practical for the future than a trip to visit friends around the world?!

6. Get informed: Knowledge makes you happy

An intelligent person finds the best education when he travels. We learn best when we see it and experience it with our eyes. We don't learn from books, from our teachers, or our parents on a trip. On our way, we experience knowledge. When we jump from sights to museums or art galleries, we collect the most memorable memories and the most lasting knowledge. After our travels, we point out our newly acquired knowledge and remember everything that has a lasting effect, and allow others to share our knowledge.

7. Get adventurous: Adventurers accomplish great things

Even if we don't believe in ourselves to be brave, everyone has a different way of doing something bold. Do you remember how exciting it was the first time you went down a mountain on skis? Did you snorkel for the first time and saw fish in all bright colours? Or the first time you ride on a plane? Have you dared to do more since then? For some, being brave means climbing a mountain, jumping out of an aircraft, or feeding sharks. For others, being bold means leaving the house and taking a trip. But in the end, anyone who dares to try something new is brave.

Travel for Experience

New shoes or a newly bought dress, not to mention the latest iPhone, make us feel good, happy, and maybe even fulfilled. But for how long? In a very short space of time, in fact, the "habit" of owning that property will make us lose even the initial sense of happiness linked to it.

For this reason, it is much better to ensure lasting happiness, to use one's money to "pay for" experiences rather than things: travel, museum visits, theatre performances, sports activities, a music course, or a seminar. In fact, all these experiences are certainly obviously accessible in exchange for money, but they do not create "habit." They are new experiences, and they are invaluable.

Travelling, for example, allows us to see new places, try different foods, meet unknown people. All this leaves within us a feeling of happiness destined to last over time and that, besides, we can "relive" every time we share it with someone through photos, stories, or simple memories. The same is true for all experiences of this type: visiting a museum or attending an opera are events that will make us feel richer and truly privileged.

Travel is Therapy

This has personally happened to me many times in Southeast Asia. Maybe aboard a train that sped through Thailand or aboard a sleeping bus that took me from Laos to Cambodia in the middle of the night. Those moments of peace and silence after a whole day spent exploring the unknown are perfect for doing what you have been putting off for a long, long time: thinking about your life, finding solutions to your problems, and starting to move towards your happiness.

It was just as the landscape darted in front of my slightly lucid eyes, with my head resting on the window of a bus and some "right" songs in my ears, that I developed the best reflections on the things of life. Those were the moments when I came to important conclusions and made difficult but necessary decisions. In those moments, I understood what form my happiness took, which paths I had to follow and which ones to avoid.

Travelling will not solve your problems. It doesn't have this power. On the other hand, travelling is an extraordinary opportunity to judge your life, experiences, and choices with a state of mind free from conditioning.

Travelling is a therapy that will allow you to make the biggest changes in your life if approached in the most conscious way possible.

Travel to observe your life from the outside because only an Experience can make that happen!

If it is true that travelling does not solve your problems, I am convinced that it has a usefulness that few people realize: it offers you the unique opportunity to observe your life from a different, external point of view. This is because every trip is unique, but all trips have one thing in common: they take you out of your comfort zone.

When you travel, you have no reference points. You don't have a place that you know perfectly well; there isn't your bedroom, bed, favourite supermarket, TV show, shopping centre, family, and friends. You have to rebuild your habits and routines from scratch, but if you travel from one location to another, you don't have the material time to do it.

This gives you a great opportunity to observe yourself, observe your habits, observe your mindset from an external point of view.

Action Items before you move to the next chapter:

• Make a list of your possessions from the last 2-4 years (Mobile Phones/Laptop/Car, etc)

• Make a list of your good experiences from the last 2-6 years (Travel, Good Relationships, Friends trip, etc)

• Think about each item on each list for 2 mins and compare the feelings of happiness felt between both the lists.

• Make a note about what you felt and you will know which type of a list excites you.

CHAPTER TWELVE

YOUR AGE IS A DEPRECIATING GIFT!

Before heading onto our topic today, let's get a deeper look into the actual meaning of the terms Age & Depreciating.

What is Age & Aging?

Aging is attributed to a lot of factors like physical health & endurance, the mingling factor, which is how well you can adapt to various things or people for that sake. And all that points to a state: wherein the peak lies in the young adulthood frame in the numerical context of age.

Well, we all might have heard that "Age is just a number." To the greatest context, it's true, for individuals with kid-like innocent mindsets. But, due to some in-elastic experiences in our lives, most of us tend to become prone to early aging, meaning: making it less exciting, losing out the enthusiasm & energy.

Thus, making the most out of your energy at different life-stages is encouraged to give a sense of satisfaction &

having the feeling of experiencing life in all modes & colours.

Now, what does "Depreciating" mean, and how does it relate to life?

The most relatable context would be: you might have heard of depreciating assets in the finance domain. They are the assets, your valuables, that lose value as they age, i.e., time passes & their values get reduced. A simple example is the Machinery of a factory, first of all, it's surely an asset as it contributes to the production & hence profits & also has a Sell-Value.

The more years it's used, the more prone it to wearing & tearing due to constant use & thus, when we set out to sell it back again for raising funds, we get less price than what we bought it for or compared to its previous value.

"In a similar light, our life is like a beautiful asset given to us, but as we age, various factors like energy, health, etc. get deteriorating, which is very much natural & uncontrollable. Hence, we can say it's a depreciating gift in nature."

One such way to redeem this wonderful present on time is to explore & take risks as much as one can while being young. We can do this by gathering as many varied experiences by means of **travelling & meeting new & different kinds of people.**

The reasons for doing it are when you're young you have the following things:

1. Physical ability: We all know that there would come one day when we can't live independently; when we can no longer drive a car; when we'll forget familiar names; when health begins to fail; when we can't walk stairs or control the bladder. But, fortunately for most of us, these won't be hurdles or problems for us when we are young. So, ensure that you actually live gathering cherishable memories while you could still physically. And to experience all the adventure activities that require physical endurance, it's best & most enjoyable to try them when young.

2. Risk-taking traits, Open to thrills: When you're young, when you have less to lose, all that you can do is go after that shining opportunity without much thought.

3. Warm Hormones- Biologically Healthy & proactive: In youth, we all know our respective growth rates & similar biological metrics are at their peaks, & harnessing the energy of that phase will surely set you apart in your career & personality domains. The preferential percentages of being fearless, instinctive action-taking, dynamic, brave are relatively higher.

4. Less Aging-related problems: As rewarding as the wisdom gained through aging, some undeniable things happen to us: Illness, Fatigue, Uncontrolled diabetes, blood pressure or other medical condition, Muscle weakness, Depression, Financial hardship, Conflict, Functional decline, loss of mobility, loss, grief, forgetfulness, memory loss, Battle of the bulge, Stress, Gray hair, glasses, wrinkles. Feeling those good years are gone, nothing to look forward to in life. Stop yourself from having such regret by "Doing all that you can by while your body allows" - Best examples would be sporty, adventurous activities like Hiking, Paragliding, etc.

5. Creativity & Adaptability - A Must for Unplanned plans: Tell me who doesn't love surprises? There's no doubt that no matter how much we plan, sudden situations occur while things might not go on the trip as we plan them. Maybe your hotel booking gets cancelled, or the weather becomes unsuitable; it would be more bearing when you're physically & mentally prepared to go out of comfort & still be on the enjoyable trip track.

6. Trip of a Tech-savvy: Travelling nowadays as you can perceive has become a sort of more planned & safer activity due to the Technologies connecting us & all the options we have. And so to get all those cool discount offers, checking out various apps, discovering all those latest trendy cultures & practices would be fun to savour with pals. When young, you have the zeal & the will to put in the efforts of participating in various weird contests like the Selfie League or Fun Jams & win those free or discount trips.

7. Travelling is important!: Nothing more is true. Precisely for this reason, I am and will remain convinced that everyone should at least try once in their life to travel backpacking. Indeed, I think that young people should be "forced" by schools and families to travel and experience abroad.

You leave your comfort zone!

We all create a comfort zone, and that's good and right. Being close to your parents or feeling part of a stable community or group of friends. Having planned activities, passions or routines.

We feel safe, secure, and at ease, and it's nice to feel that way, but Getting used to ALWAYS living in our comfort zone is wrong. Convenient, true, but wrong.

First of all, sooner or later, something will happen in our life that will tear us away from our comfort zone. Having never experimented in small steps, we will find ourselves overwhelmed by events without having the tools and skills to deal with them. Secondly, as many professionals with whom I fully share the thought affirm, leaving your comfort zone is synonymous with Personal Growth, even if this must take place gradually and with the right resources.

Initially, we can feel scared, lost. Still, once we learn how to move in diversity and address unknown people and other cultures, we will be more competent, more emotionally intelligent people.

Test yourself, face uncomfortable situations, because it will help you become a better person than you already are now.

Travelling increases self-esteem!

Starting from the simplest things like understanding which means to get to a given place, or having to ask someone who does not speak our language for information, helps build our self-esteem, adapt to what surrounds us, and what is there: Unknown.

This is precisely one of the greatest lessons that travel can give us. The fact of discovering things that we already have within us but that we have never had to bring out, hiding them from ourselves.

You cannot imagine how many times, in my travels, I have been told: "What courage you have" or "But how can you travel alone for months? I could never do it". And every time I find myself answering something like this:

It's simple actually, really, and anyone can do it. It is not true that you cannot do it, you do not WANT to do it!

Travelling opens up new horizons!

Everything we know about the other is our fantasy, a partial perception of reality, often our interpretation of interpretations that are told to us by others, whether they are people, media, or otherwise.

Do stereotypes tell you something? We all tend to trivialize, to simplify, cultures and people different from ours, labelling them.

An example (rather stupid but which gives the idea) is that of Japanese food. Just ask: "What do the Japanese eat?", Answer: "Sushi." True, they eat it, but they don't just eat sushi or sashimi; on the contrary, they only eat it occasionally. They eat rice, spaghetti, soups, chicken, pork cutlets, etc., more often like us.

Trivial example but which can make you understand immediately what we are talking about. There would be thousands of other examples to consider more seriously.

The journey allows us to discover new truths, new traditions, and ideals, which in addition to culturally increase us to clarify doubts or perplexities about events that we just cannot understand.

Learning to observe things from multiple points of view is a rare and wonderful skill.

Knowing the truth that your age is a depreciating gift!

Travelling young and learning as it is an adventure that gives you new stimuli every day, helps you grow your energy and enthusiasm that you will cherish when you are old. It gives me joy and hopes that when we grow old, and our numbers start depreciating, we will have built immense memories to fill our hearts in our old age!

When I look at the future, I can see how we will find peace and harmony even though we will grow weaker physically. Still, I am convinced emotionally we will have inner peace, and we will have diverse stories to share with our generations. I see how we will grow in the fraternity, attention to others, and respect for different experiences and various points of view. This age or moment is a celebration because we have opportunities to see the world, travel now & grow hopes and dreams for the future.

Travel Memories Remain Forever with Us!

The memories of the trips we take remain with us for our entire life and influence our life.

But why are travel memories so important?

When we travel, we find ourselves outside our everyday life; we have a different mood, we focus on different aspects than those we are used to. We, therefore, associate the journey with positive emotions. We remember the episodes of the journey and not the facts, and the human mind likes the episodes and the stories.

We will hardly remember the monuments or museums, but rather the natural landscapes, the smells, the flavours, the food, and friendly human relations. And all these memories come back to our minds when we least expect it, they come back and make us feel good, they make us happy just like when we were travelling.

Travel memories are tasty!

The food memories are around 40.9% so let's look for my tasty memories! I perfectly remember the taste and smell of lobsters that I ate while travelling to Bali! I remember the colour of that dish, the beauty, and the flavour! I think I've never eaten a fish dish as good as that, and if I go back, I think I'd go back there to eat the same dish!

Travel memories are fragrant!

Often flavours and smells come together and intersect. You hardly remember the taste and not the smell, at least for me it is! But there are also smells that remain impressed on you and that if you smell them by chance, they bring you back in a moment to that place and at that moment.

We love the road very much precisely because they allow us to discover cities and landscapes. For example, we often go to the discovery of scenic roads... not so much the destination but also the road!

Memories of a young age are not simple things; they are fragrances that enter you and give you such strong emotions that you cannot forget even when your age depreciates!

When you have travelled in your youth, It revitalizes your physical and mental health when you are old. Believe me, age is just a number, and when you grow in numbers, your best memories of your travel will fill your life when you move on to "old age." The skills and lessons you learned from your past travels will spin the globe in your memories when your backpacking days are over!

Travelling for long periods or studying abroad offers a further, enormous advantage. Learn a new language, and experience new things today that you may not experience tomorrow. Not only is learning a new language an excellent exercise for our mind, but it will give space, in the future, to many new opportunities, work and otherwise, that without that journey we would never have been able to have. Since your age is depreciating, consider it ideal when you are young, start travelling and build up foundations for the future. As travel gives you wisdom, and when you are old, it always keeps you young at the heart!

Fortunately, you are still alive!

If you are reading this, I can pretty much be sure that you are alive! (Pun Intended)! I believe that life itself is the greatest gift irrespective of what we have in our materialistic world. If you are not in a hospital/prison or cemetery, I think you are good. Rest can be managed somehow. But to develop this mindset, you need to feel that your life is limited and better than most.

When you travel young and realize that everyone has very limited time on this earth, you do things differently. You do not run behind things that will just take away your energy and make you realize they are not worth it. When you realize that your age is limited and life is uncertain, you will do things that matter today, not tomorrow, or 10 years down the line. Sure, everything you do today can also be heading towards your goals in the future, but not living today for tomorrow is the worst excuse you can give yourself.

So I would just like to plant this seed in your head that you are allowed to live today, you are allowed to be happy today and enjoy the very limited life you have here before you realize that things you always wanted were held for the future, which never came!

CHAPTER THIRTEEN

WE TAKE ONLY MEMORIES WHEN WE DIE

Memories, good and bad, tell the story of your life. They gently or achingly remind you of the paths you've taken, the people you've cherished, and the choices you've selected.

Memories gives you the power to not lose an image, a sound, or a touch from your mind. You can bring memories to life on-demand, and the more times you do so, the more permanence you give to a moment. It's the closest thing we humans have to stop time.

Why would I have to spend money in memories — can't I get them for free?

It's true; some of the best memories don't cost us anything monetarily. Despite that, we're still spending money throughout our lives on stuff and more stuff — it never ends. Houses, cars, travel, concerts, home improvements, food, even utilities. Why not focus some of your money on goods, services, and experiences that will produce good memories to grow old with?

You probably won't derive many good memories from paying your electric bill, but have you thought about the other things you're throwing money towards?

Let's look at something that usually takes a lot of money, the home. I hope your home is producing good memories for you. Through sharing your home with loved ones, raising children, planting gardens, or warm fires on cold winter evenings, we can hopefully say it is money well spent.

What do you remember the most about your childhood? A game your parents bought you a birthday present? Or was it the experience of your birthday party and of playing the game? The truth is, most of our favorite memories are built off of the experiences we've had, usually with other people!

And, since science tells us that remembering good memories makes us happier, we've got to keep making good memories to look back on. Hence, we gotta travel more! Let's go through all the other reasons why traveling is far better for our happiness than just accumulating material wealth!

We need to share happiness with people to be happy truly.

Believe it or not, loneliness can be a real danger to our health! It's not only bad for us to be alone, but it's almost just as bad to feel lonely. Sometimes being in the same environment for too long can forget to appreciate the people around us or not experiencing true community. That's when it's time for an adventure abroad!

When we travel, we're stepping outside of our norm into the unknown. And because we need to feel secure when we're in an unfamiliar place, we tend to be more open-minded and trusting when making friends abroad. That's why a lot of meaningful and long-lasting connections are often made on the road. You'll also grow a lot closer to those you travel with.

Robert Waldinger's Harvard study shares that loneliness can have the same damaging effect on us as smoking or alcoholism. Another member of the research team, George Valliant, also explains in his book "Aging Well," "the key to healthy aging is relationships, relationships, relationships."

Isn't that so true? We tend to experience happiness when remembering the moments we've had with friends and family throughout our lives. Even just one good experience with people we meet at a faraway place can bring us joy for the rest of our lives every time we recall those memories!

Travelling improves our emotional and mental health.

Whether we're travelling either just for a vacation or for an enriching cultural-exchange experience, it liberates us. Studies have shown that the exciting sensations of travelling expands our mind and transforms the way we think! So the more you travel, the better it is for your mental health, especially if you put down the phone for a bit to live in each moment.

At home, we often get tied to our phones and forget to live in the here and now. Travel takes us outside the box of what we've grown accustomed to and helps us break out of our routines, including bad habits of compulsively checking our phone and logging into social media every other minute.

While we know, it's not always feasible to unplug completely, and it's worth trying to cut down your screen time as much as possible. Research shows that this can turn out to be mentally freeing!

Science direct links experiences with happiness.

Ever wondered why when you first see something new and shiny, it's all you could've ever wanted...until it's not? The more we buy, the more we want, whereas experiences become memories, we'll almost always get to keep. These memories stay with us over the years and age with us as we grow! What we experience also gives us a brighter outlook on life while becoming the stories we tell when we're older.

Dr. Thomas Gilovich, a psychology professor at Cornell University, recently explained to the world in his research how happiness is directly linked with experiences and not material possessions:

"One of the enemies of happiness is adaptation. We buy things to make us happy, and we succeed. But only for a while. New things are exciting to us at first, but then we adapt to them."

As we get used to the things we buy, the excitement and happiness fade, and things become mundane until we find our next object of desire to fill our void temporarily, to repeat the cycle all over again! And then we're just left with this emptiness that often comes with just having a bunch of stuff we'd eventually throw away or leave behind. Why not go on a trip instead of immersing ourselves in the world around us and experience life more fully?! It's been done before, with beautiful results!

So, travelling's not just better than material possessions but helps us improve our overall health, wellbeing, and happiness. Happiness is not what we buy, but how we live. Wondering where to start making new memories? Here are some amazing experiences you could give a go! Keep making happy travel memories, nomads!

Why You Should Travel While You're Young At Any Cost?

Talking about travel has become such a source of currency since I began taking these trips. I've found that even when you come from different walks of life or are drastically different ages, discussing a trip can become a wonderful common ground. Job interviewers always ask me about my time in travelling the world—it's usually the aspect of my life they've focused the most on and been the most interested in. Even at a dinner party or on a date, travel stories are the ones I'm most likely to draw on to make myself a little more interesting.

While deciding whether or not to travel, I wasn't always thinking, "How can this trip add to my professional and personal value?" Most of the time, I was thinking, "I want to travel while I'm young. I'm ready for another adventure." But I've been pleasantly surprised with the results.

For me, it's gaining a sense of confidence I would never have had otherwise. I know myself, both my strengths and weaknesses, as I never could some years ago. Because on all of these adventures, only one thing remained consistent—me. And it's valuable to see how I've reacted to all the circumstances I've found myself in.

If you don't believe me, take it from the experts.

I love this quote from a book called "A Hat Full of Sky." In it, the author Terry Pratchett writes, "Why do you go away? So that you can come back. So that you can see the place you came from with new eyes and extra colors. And the people there see you differently, too. Coming back to where you started is not the same as never leaving."

Or, as Mark Twain wrote more famously, "Travel is fatal to prejudice, bigotry, and narrow-mindedness, and many of our people need it sorely on these accounts. Broad, wholesome, charitable views of men and things cannot be acquired by vegetating in one little corner of the earth all one's lifetime."

I've gotten a lot of wanderlust out of my system in just a few years. What makes me happiest is, I don't think I'll look back and say, "I should have."

I know taking this approach is risky. I do feel fortunate that it has worked out for me thus far. But if you can make travel work while you're young—and do it responsibly—there are ways it can pay for itself.

Incredible Reasons To Travel When You're Young

- It will help you decide what you want in life.

It is common in human nature not to know what you like until you experiment with it. Travelling when young can be a great platform to diversify your experience early in life and discover your purpose in life. Each country, each city, even each restaurant you might visit is an opportunity to experiment with something different. It is better to realize your true desires and potential early in life rather than realize them when you think it's too late.

- Fewer physical attachments equal more freedom.

As you grow, you start to settle your life with physical attachments like a mortgage, a car, and kids. Travelling before this stage of your life will be much easier, and the freedom will be priceless. You will be able to travel for longer terms, more often, and with fewer preoccupations.

- You learn how to manage your money early in life.

There is nothing worse than being out on the road and run out of money. You feel like you're lost and that the world is about to end. There is no financial comfort zone when you're travelling; everything depends on you.

For that reason, traveling serves as a great "teaching lesson" to manage your finances. How so? Well, if you spend recklessly, you'll see its effect on subsequent parts of your trip.

- You'll get street smart.

It's always good to compliment your "school smart" with some "street smart," and there's no better way to do this than travelling. Travelling teaches you a wide variety of things that can be applied to your daily life –from the banalest to the most indispensable. When travelling, you acquire unique wisdom that is useful for your entire life.

- It will make you a more interesting person.

There is nothing more compelling than having a conversation with someone who has something to say. You will not be a blank canvas anymore; your travels will be part of your story as a person. Travelling creates an exciting story in your life that is worthy of telling to all your friends. Not only your travel conversations can be of great interest, but they can also be eye-openers to other people.

- You'll grow culturally.

Be it a different way of living, a religion, or simply anything foreign to you, when you travel, and you get exposed to different cultures that can have a direct impact on your life. Your tolerance will grow as you experiment with them, and in many cases, you'll learn how to see things from a different perspective. Every culture is different and so is every person in it.

- You'll learn to develop your independence and how to be responsible.

Travelling is one of the best ways to learn how to be independent. When you travel, everything relies on you. Even if you travel on an organized trip, you have to exert a certain degree of organizational skills, responsibility, and independence. When travelling independently, you are responsible for your plane tickets, accommodations, transportation, passport, and money —it's like a crash course of life.

- Travel provides an opportunity to expand your friendships.

In everyday life, the security and consistency of the friendship circles you have grown up with make it hard to find the motivation to go out and meet new people. It suddenly becomes so much easier to open yourself up and meet new, interesting people once you are out traveling the world. Expanding your friendships is invaluable, and let's be honest, you aren't going to make many new friends by buying designer heels.

- Travel gives you more stories to tell your grandkids than a new iPhone will

Guess what? That iPhone 6S you spent hundreds of dollars on ain't going to impress your future grandkids. They will laugh at such an ancient artefact. Do you know what might impress them? That time you saw the pyramids in Egypt.

When you went sky diving over the Swiss Alps. The experience you had trekking through the Himalayas. Stop collecting meaningless things and start collecting some awesome stories!

- *Possessions will constantly let you down and will not last.*

Material objects break, get lost, or become obsolete. There are many ways that something we once loved can let us down and become a source of frustration. Sure, travelling doesn't always go as per plan, but even the mishaps and setbacks when you travel add to the experience and are the things you'll laugh about later on. Your smashed iPhone, on the other hand – not so much.

- *You won't resent it later in life.*

There is nothing worse than reaching a later stage in life and regretting not doing something when you were young. Well, traveling is one of those. There are many things to experience in this world, so why wait till later in life to enjoy them? There is no reason to spend your active young years just working. As they say, don't live to work... work to live.

- *Because you deserve it!*

Hell yeah! We all deserve to have a good time travelling and to see what's out there. There is no need to wait until later in life to start experiencing the world. Don't let the opportunity pass you by, explore the world while you're young!

Travel memories change your life. Science says so!

"We humans are what we memorize in the course of our life"

Travel memories have such an intense effect that they stay with us for life. But how are travel memories imprinted on our memory? How do they differ from other memories? And how do they affect us?

Travel has become an increasingly necessary element for our mind. When we travel, we find ourselves outside of our everyday life, we have a different mood, we focus on various aspects than those we are used to, and we are free to do so. We, therefore, associate the journey with positive emotions. We remember the journey episodes and not the facts, and the human mind likes the episodes and the stories.

Our personality is formed through travel: relationships with others change when we travel. The most important aspect of human memories is that we are what we memorize in our lives. Our memories thus influence our past, that we learn a lot from our experiences. We remember people, places, even food. This is nothing new: artists, writers, and intellectuals traveled already 200 years ago to train and receive an education. Today it still is. And it is for all of us.

But what do people remember about the trips they take? "When we return from a trip, we don't remember everything we saw, but the mind can fix some details. Certain sensory stimuli ignite in us "flashbulb memories" that make us relive the holidays. We don't remember monuments but natural landscapes. We recognize the scents, the noises of nature, such as the chirping of birds, for example, aspects that we would never give importance to in everyday life.

The environments we see influence our memories, and the reason is straightforward: we must remember that we too are social animals and, like animals, we are attracted to natural places. We will not forget all our lives to have seen the greenery, to have seen the ocean, because it is nature that attracts us, with its smells, not things. When we smell a particular perfume, we immediately associate it with an experience we had in the past, and it reminds us of the event, making us change our mood.

So here is what I will recommend you to do to make your trips unforgettable.

During a trip:

1. Take 5 to 10 minutes every day to savour a situation or a moment of your journey with awareness;

2. When you visit a place, imagine stories that take place right there.

3. Keep a travel journal.

4. Send yourself a postcard.

After the trip:

5. Read a book set in your travel destination.

6. Buy a planisphere and mark the places you have visited;

7. Prepare a "travel box".

8. Talk about your experiences with fellow travellers.

With these simple rules, we can best preserve our travel memories for a lifetime!

CHAPTER FOURTEEN

LIFE IS CERTAIN. DEATH IS NOT

You might have always heard that famous quote by Augustus Hill 'Death is Certain and Life is not' but contradictory to what the majority think; I believe you have more control over the actions you do in life rather what you can do about your death.

If you are not dead, you are alive and kicking, and that's what this chapter is all about. This is about making a point that we have limited life which could be anything we want (at least up to certain possibilities). When we are alive, we forget about trivial things we have for which some people dream about.

There are millions without limbs, millions without eyesight, millions with disabilities, and many more with a lack of basic food and hygiene. But how many of us who do not have these problems cherish our life differently? Very Few! Humans are hard-wired to always think about what we want next and what we can do better or how we can move forward in each and everything. Be it a career, relationship, studies, business, or skill set, we want to improvise and move towards doing better.

While nothing is wrong with that, we should not forget what we already have, what we can already cherish. If nothing else, we always have our life to be grateful for. If you are reading this and have a roof over your head, you already have something to cherish for.

We are all going to die – it's a sure thing, but aren't we living for sure till we die? A question we all should think about. I always believe that remembering death every day or just acknowledging it every day makes us live much more lively. I know it's ironic to lead happy life thinking about death. But just think of it, why do some people have never-ending greed as there is no end? Why do some people hurt others to have more money, more things? Why do some children con their own parents into giving up materialistic things?

Do you think these people ever think of death? Do you think these people see life as limited time? I don't think so. Many people, including us, sometimes think we have enough time in life, we have infinity to live, so we make our decisions based on these internal thoughts. But what if you start thinking the opposite? What if you start thinking that death is something that can come any day, any time, but what we are not sure about is how much amazing time we have left on earth? How much time do we have to be fully happy? How much do we have for our parents, kids, family, and friends and do all the beautiful things we always wanted to do?

I think people who enjoy travelling are the same people who generally enjoy life more than others because to be a traveller (Not a wishful thinker), you really need to know your priorities in life. Many people who do not understand travelling say the money is purely wasted on travelling; instead, it can buy cars, iPhones, etc. But this chapter or even this book is not about those people; this book is about people who always had traveller spirit inside them somewhere to be unleashed.

Coming back to the same point, people who enjoy travelling are well matured enough to understand that life is limited and they need to see what amazing beauty the world has to offer, what unique people and cultures this world has to offer and even with the full efforts, you will never see or experience everything in the world.

Not Knowing Everything Keeps Us Alive

When we start the journey of life, we are always learning something new. We are learning from how to speak to how to walk, from how to use computers to specific skills. Learning is something that never stops, and that basically keeps us going.

Would you pick up the Kinder Garden book and keep enjoying reading ABC again and again? Of course not. Once you learn the characters, you move to spelling, then to sentences, then to reading and writing, and so on. It's a continuous process till we die. The reason you won't enjoy doing the same thing or learning the same things, again and again, is that we are hard-wired to evolve. Humanity is made of a fundamental rule: evolution. You cannot stop growing even if you want to. You will always be one day older tomorrow than today; that's how evolution works.

So when we know something, we want to know something else. When we are skilled in something, we want to be better than yesterday to do our jobs quicker. When we learn something, we want to try having its application in the real world. So we consistently work on something and keep moving forward. If we ever feel we know everything, we lose interest in doing anything more, so go out and know what you still don't know. Trust me, there are millions of things you don't know, and the most interesting part is that you don't know what you don't know.

Life is Certain

When we are born, we do not know how much time we have in life. We may die the next day, or we may live up to 100 years and more. But doesn't that make life uncertain? Maybe or Maybe not. It depends on how you look at it.

When I say life is certain, I do not intend that we are sure of our lives, but I intend to say that we are sure to move forward and continue to live against all odds as long as we are alive. When we are faced against extreme odds like the Covid Pandemic, and Dangers of all sorts, we still move forward doing our things. So as long as we do our things despite knowing that death can hit us the next day, aren't we sure of living till we die? In a way, we are certain that whatever we are doing now is making sense to us, is having some meaning for us, or else why would you do anything at all?

Personally, when I wake up in the morning, I always smile in gratitude to have another beautiful day on this earth. As long as I will live today, I will do what I want, which makes me believe in the illusional certainty of the present moment. This illusion or a feeling of gratitude gives me hope to take out my daily routine in a blissful way, thinking that whatever I am doing today, I am certain to do so, and while doing whatever I am, why not enjoy the time I have.

This may all sound weird but if you live in a moment and enjoy it, you will always feel that life is more certain than death.

Death is Not

Death may be the most inevitable thing for each of us, but it is certain only for a moment. Before that moment, your life is still alive and kicking. To put this into perspective, why do people with Cancer still play games, read books, or even create new ventures? If they are so sure of death, maybe more than us, they should give it all up and just wait to die, right? But we do not do that because we live our life till we are alive and face death only when it comes for us.

Even in all surety that one day we will face that moment, we do not give death that weightage of certainty, or else life would become lifeless, and everyone would just wait for it to be over. But knowing this all will end for us one day, we all live and do millions of things in our life, not because death is not certain, but because we cannot stop living when we are alive.

I think everything we do in life gets meaning because we know that the time we have is limited, and if we want to do what we love, we have to make choices, and when we make choices, we stay on a single path or a single option and does not know what would have happened if we would have chosen something else. I think that is the most beautiful thing about being mortal. So when I write this paragraph, it makes an impression that we all know that death is not inevitable, but at least we know we should make choices that will make our life worth it for ourselves.

So when you find meaning in whatever you do, doesn't it make it more solid and certain rather than a thing like death which is not in our control in any form? Think about it!

I would like to end this book with a thought that whatever we do, whatever we feel, we find meaning in it, and the best way to give meaning to our actions and thoughts is to travel young when your mind is open to accepting new realities of the world and have more acceptance for everything.

When you travel the world under 30 or at a young age, your eyes and other senses are in accepting mode and want to perceive new things to make meaning out of what you see, listen to, and understand. You understand that life is beautiful, limited, and with endless possibilities. You also understand that there is nothing right or wrong in this world; these terms are just made of actions/thoughts of our surroundings and culture. If you give new meaning to the same action, your perception of right to wrong or wrong to right will change tremendously.

I wish you all the best for your physical as well as a spiritual journey in this world and I would always ask you to explore this beautiful world and glorious life as much as you can!

Acknowledgements

I never imagined in my wildest dreams that one day I would be writing this page, let alone writing my own book on travelling. But as they say, you will never find out if you never try, so here we are. With the Covid-19 Pandemic, we all got time to retrospect about what we want to do with life which brings out more meaning to us and others around us. This book is one of those realisations which happened to me in the middle of the Pandemic. For the first time, I had time to contemplate how I can make my experiences useful to others, how I can inspire more people to try the life I have lived and how I can put it all together in one place. Finally, with the help of the internet and the support of my people, I have tried to write this book as best as I can.

Without the awesome people I met around the world and the overwhelming support of my parents, peers, and friends to take risks, this life I have lived or the book you are reading wouldn't exist. I am grateful for all the people I met on my journey and all the great people who supported me. **Especially, Thanks to my parents, Gordhan Golani and Alka Golani, for always being there for my crazy dreams and supporting them to the fullest. Thanks to my wife, Ekta Golani, for always pushing me to be the best version of myself and being there with all the answers I need. I would also like to appreciate my best buddies, Rajendra Singh Rohra and Paresh Khatri for giving me all the clarity in the world when most needed, which helped me in writing and completing this book.**

I want to thank each and every one of you who has read this book because it means the world to me as a person and as a first-time writer. I would always be grateful if this book changed the life of even one person and helped them explore this beautiful world in a better way. I would always be happy to help with anything related to this book. You can reach me at devgolani@gmail.com

About The Author

Devesh Golani

After realizing that most young people find travelling luxurious and unnecessarily expensive, Devesh Golani has given himself out to break this stereotype, encouraging and inspiring them to travel and to explore the world extensively before the age of 30. Devesh is an upcoming author, Blogger, Quality Assurance Engineer, Web Developer, and an avid Traveller with a great propensity to share travelling ideas on his travel blog Wanderlust Planet. Partly, he also drives his inspiration from travelling around 40 countries before age 30, something he believes every youth can accomplish.

Through the book, he simplifies the travelling process and encourages people to travel to as many countries as possible to learn about new cultures, meet new people and learn new things in life. He also artistically deconstructs the myth that travelling requires a lot of money and time. Instead, he displays it as a simple thing that only needs planning and ambition.

Currently, Devesh Golani lives in Mumbai, India. He is an avid traveller and has a passion for developing websites and hacking systems. Owing to his avid readership culture, he tries to read at least 3-4 books a month.

If you have enjoyed this book or learned anything or need help related to travel, you can reach out to him at devgolani@gmail.com | Feedback is always important for a first-time writer!